Seeking Spiritual Growth
through the Bible

Seeking Spiritual Growth through the Bible

Wilfrid J. Harrington, O.P.

PAULIST PRESS
New York   Mahwah, N.J.

ROBERT J. WICKS
A
Spirituality Selection

Book design by Theresa M. Sparacio and Lynn Else

Cover design by Cynthia Dunne

Library of Congress Cataloging-in-Publication Data

Harrington, Wilfrid J.
   Seeking spiritual growth through the Bible / Wilfrid J. Harrington.
     p. cm.
   Includes bibliographical references.
   ISBN 0-8091-3999-5 (alk. paper)
   1. Spirituality–Biblical teaching. I. Title.

BS680.S7 H37 2001
291.4–dc21

                                    2001054583

Published by Paulist Press
997 Macarthur Boulevard
Mahwah, New Jersey 07430

www.paulistpress.com

Printed and bound in the
United States of America

CONTENTS

PREFACE

he theme of this book is biblical spirituality. Both terms
need to be pondered. *Spirituality*, in current usage, carries
a bewilderingly wide connotation. Here, *spirituality* is understood
as *faith*, lived in *love*, sustained by *hope*. Our plan, consequently,
is straightforward: We follow that trajectory. We look to the Bible's
witness. In view of the differences between the Testaments, we
take, in turn, the Old Testament—the Scripture of Israel—and the
New Testament. Because the whole is Christian Scripture, there is
a natural overlap. In view of the scope and modest length of the
book, our reading of the Bible is necessarily quite selective.

Faith. Our faith is trust in God. We must learn that the God in
whom we trust is wondrous, a God of *infinite* love and mercy and
forgiveness. We find this God in the Scripture of Israel. His graciousness has been fully revealed in and through the Son. God is
now a visible God, if we permit Jesus Christ to image him, if we do
let Jesus have *his* say.

Love. Christian life is faith-inspired life. It is a Way marked by
love—love of God and of one another. It is a *koinōnia*—fellowship:
"Our fellowship is with the Father and with his Son Jesus Christ"
(1 John 1:3). This asks of us that we strive to see others as our sisters and brothers, all alike beloved children of the one Parent. By
our Lord we are called to discipleship and are challenged to bear
witness. Our faith-life must be fueled by prayer.

Hope. Our Christian life is pilgrimage; we need to be sure that
we do not journey toward a mirage. Our comfort: "We have this
hope, a sure and steadfast anchor of the soul" (Heb 6:19). Our
hope, like our faith, is based on the faithfulness of our God, the
God we meet in the Son. Our star of hope shines for us beyond
suffering, beyond death itself. This is why we run with perseverance the race that is set before us. We look to our role model—
"looking to Jesus the pioneer and perfecter of our faith, who for

1

the sake of the joy that was set before him endured the cross, disregarding its shame, and has taken his seat at the right hand of the throne of God" (12:2). Our striving is to become truly children of God, to become authentically human. We can dare to hope that, at the end, a loving Parent will be merciful to all.

In the writing of this book I have come to recognize that my spirituality is, undoubtedly, biblical. I am content that it is so. I had, at times, tended to feel that I may be hopelessly optimistic. Now I prefer to regard myself as realistically hopeful.

INTRODUCTION

SPIRITUALITY

*I*n current usage, *spirituality* is a broad and elusive term. At its most general it involves a reflection on human development. Human beings are spirit in the world: a paradoxical condition. Spirituality is the lived experience of that dimension. As an activity of human life it is available to any man or woman who is seeking to live an authentically human life. Spirituality has been defined as: "The experience of consciously striving to integrate one's life in terms not of isolation and self-absorption but of self-transcendence toward the ultimate value one perceives."[1] It is a lived experience determined by the nature of the particular ultimate value. In light of that value, one seeks personal integration through reaching beyond the confines of the self. In this sense, spirituality is the endeavor to arrive at a more authentic and richer human life. In short, spirituality, as a lived experience, is an activity of human life as such. While not necessarily defined by religion, spirituality is regularly envisaged in relation to religion. In that case the ultimate value is divine.

In Israel the ultimate concern was God, revealed in creation and liberating intervention (the Exodus), and experienced through God's presence in Word and Spirit and Wisdom, within the life of God's people. In Christianity the ultimate value is God revealed in Jesus Christ and experienced through the gift of the Holy Spirit within the life of the Church. The believing Israelite and the believing Christian strove and strive to live a life motivated by the experienced presence of God. Biblical spirituality is the Bible's witness to this striving, its witness to the lived faith and hope of the people of Israel and of the first followers of the Christian Way. This book will offer some instances. More significantly, that same biblical spirituality may be seen as an inspiration to us who seek to walk that Way. We may in some fashion integrate it into our own lived faith. A study of spirituality ought not remain abstract or academic. It should offer help in our own spiritual striving and equip us to foster the spiritual lives of others.

The Scripture of Israel

In considering *biblical* spirituality we need to advert to an intriguing feature of our Christian Bible: Four-fifths of it is pre-Christian! There is, then, question of the relationship between the Testaments. One approach has been to "save" the Old Testament by reading a Christian message into all its texts, by making it, indeed, little more than a prophecy of the Christ to come. This began with the early church fathers who resorted to allegory and typology in order to define various levels of meaning. This, in effect, turned the Old Testament into a Christian book. It was stripped of a value of its own. Another approach consists in making a value judgment on the basis of New Testament teaching, which is then imposed upon the Old Testament, separating the elements of abiding value from those too "ancient, sub-Christian or outworn" to concern us. The Old Testament is seen as historically conditioned, as God's self-revelation "developing" toward Christianity. What remained tended to the "spiritualized" and moralized.

Today we take due account of the fact that the Old Testament is pre-Christian. We appreciate that the Christian must take the Old Testament seriously, not solely as a historical document that offers the background of later movements, but as a serious and vital moment for present faith and life. The Word of God to Israel should be taken for what it is, truly revelation of God, and not be too hastily Christianized.

A regular failing in Christian evaluation of the Old Testament is what is termed supersessionism—the view that the Old Testament has been superseded by the New. This assessment may be presented blatantly or in a less obvious manner. There is no doubt that the Old Testament has been used by Christians in a variety of ways to assault Jewish faith and to foster anti-Semitism. The supersessionist inclination of Christian scholarship simply kept Jewish reality off the screen of perception. This had made it nearly impossible for Christians to attend to the riches of Judaism. The truth is that while Christians may indeed say of the Old Testament: "It is ours," we must add: "It is not ours alone." It remains the Scripture of Judaism. I have long felt that the great ecumenical tragedy is not the rifts between the Christian churches but the rift between Judaism and Christianity. We would do well to recall Paul's image of the olive tree and his admonishment: "Remember that it is not you [Gentile Christians] that support the root [Israel], but the root that supports you" (Rom 11:18). Perhaps the basic ecumenical concern should be here.

A Christian interpreter should acknowledge the independent status of the Old Testament text. It is clear, for instance, that the Old Testament does not directly or obviously point to Jesus or to the New Testament. We ought, indeed, recognize and respect the connections made in the New Testament and in the subsequent Church. Christianity has discerned the connections; they are not evident in the Old Testament witness. The Old Testament carries immense value without them. A bridge has been built—but backwards, from the New Testament to the Old. The Testaments are, for Christians, firmly linked. But the intrinsic value of the Old Testament has not been superseded.

In our brief study of biblical spirituality, the Old Testament is treated with the utmost respect. While my professional leaning has been toward the New Testament, in a teaching career of over forty years I have taught Old Testament as much as New. I am grateful for the experience. I have learned much from the Old Testament. I revere and admire the God of the Old Testament—the Hebrew God. And, after all, the Old Testament was authoritative Scripture for Jesus himself, who knew no God save its God, and who found in it the key to his own mission.

FAITH IN GOD

Because the Hebrew Bible does not really have a word for faith, what we have come to term *faith* is, in the Old Testament, described rather than defined. The description, in the main, concerns the relationship of Israel to Yahweh and the relationship to

Yahweh of some key figures of Israel. In both cases the ground of faith is trust in the faithfulness of Yahweh. At its most basic, faith is that attitude which discerns God creatively in action in the world and in human life. This perception urges the commitment of oneself in trust and obedience. The faithfulness of God denotes God's fulfillment of the obligations assumed in creating humankind and, particularly, in the calling of Abraham, the choosing of Israel to be his people. Deuteronomy, repeatedly, makes clear that the choice had nothing to do with anything Israel was or had done. It was love alone that prompted God's call, and the covenant with them that made them God's people (see Deut 4:32–40; 6:10–23). God's faithfulness was shown in delivering, saving and vindicating Israel despite Israel's own failure. God is always free. And God is not predictable—except that his *hesed,* his covenant-faithfulness, endures. God is respecter of freedom.[2]

Abraham

There ought to be a faith response to God's faithfulness. We have an outstanding exemplar of response. Abraham was chosen and called—the "scandal" of divine election. He was called to serve the divine purpose, and in this service the scandal is resolved. Abraham was summoned to break with his natural ties: country, clan and family (Gen 12:1). He was to get up and go "to the land that I will show you." The author of Hebrews has a perceptive comment: "By faith Abraham obeyed when he was called and set out for a place that he was to receive as an inheritance; and he set out, not knowing where he was going" (Heb 11:8).

From the start, Abraham was a man of faith. Yahweh was fully aware of the difficulty of what was asked: Abraham must leave everything. Later, despite his advanced age and that of a barren Sarah, Abraham put his faith in Yahweh, confident that he will, somehow, be ancestor of numberless descendants (Gen 15:5–6). Then there is that "sacrifice": his readiness to sacrifice the child of promise, Isaac (22:1–19). A poignant story indeed. "Take your son, your only son Isaac, whom you love...and offer him as a burnt offering....So Abraham rose early in the morning" (22:2–3). The man who had, without hesitation, at the Lord's bidding set out from his homeland now, without question, sets out to do this awful deed. He obeyed with a heavy heart, a heart pierced to the quick by Isaac's unsuspecting question: "The fire and the wood are here, but where is the lamb for a burnt offering?" (11:7). The tragic dignity of Abraham and his readiness to give his own son stirred a Christian sentiment. The deed of Abraham has surely colored the telling of a greater love: "He who did not withhold his own Son, but gave him up for all of us" (Rom 8:32); "God so loved the world that he gave his only Son" (John 3:16). Abraham had put his faith in God, a seemingly capricious and callous God. For, Abraham saw, what Paul and John were to recognize, that his God, however unpredictable, is to be trusted. God can make outrageous demands because he will ever be faithful. As regards Abraham, the verdict of Paul stands: Abraham is a man of faith (Gal 3:6-9; Rom 4:1-3).

Paul

In the New Testament *faith (pistis)* is a key term that refers, in different ways, to salvation accomplished in Christ. It will suffice, here, to look to Paul. For Paul, faith is that attitude in which, acknowledging one's complete insufficiency and relying utterly on the sufficiency of God, one accepts the revelation and the fact of divine justification in Jesus Christ. The righteousness (*dikaiosyne*) of God is the saving deed by which God restores sinful humankind to his friendship. The life and death of Jesus and his resurrection constitute that decisive event: By his death, Christ has delivered humankind from sin and by his resurrection has won for us life in the Spirit. We are, then, justified, set right with God and accepted by him, through faith in Jesus Christ.

Paul, however, adds a special nuance. In Galatians 2:16 he declares: "We know that a person is justified not by the works of the law but through the faith of Jesus Christ." While the usual rendering is "faith *in* Jesus," "the faith *of* Jesus" is preferable. The faith of Christ is manifested in his obedience to God by his death on the cross. He had trusted himself wholly to the Father. Justification comes from and is based upon that faith of Jesus manifested upon the cross. His faith is a deed of love, a love expressed as self-sacrifice for others. This faith—faithfulness—of Jesus Christ is the ground of our faith *in* Jesus Christ. In Revelation 1:5 Jesus is characterized as "the faithful witness"—the one faithful unto death. What we might term "Christ-faith" encompasses both the faith *of* Christ and faith *in* Christ. As Christians, then, our faith is grounded not only on a faithful God but on the trustworthiness of Father *and* Son. We have reason for confidence indeed. At the end of the day, faith is our yes to God; it is letting God be God in our lives. This being so, our faith should be lived faith—lived out in love.

LOVE OF GOD AND OF HUMANKIND

"Which commandment is the first of all?" (Mark 12:28). This question of a scribe to Jesus was one the rabbis sought to answer. They looked for the commandment that outweighed all the others, one that might be regarded as the basic principle on which the whole Law was grounded. Jesus had been asked to name a commandment; he responded by naming two commandments: "'You shall love the Lord your God with all your heart, and with all your soul, and with all your strength.' The second is this, 'You shall love your neighbor as yourself.' There is no other commandment greater than these" (12:30-31). This reply is of great importance. It would seem that Jesus was the first to bring together these two commands of love of God and love of neighbor (see Deut 6:4; Lev 19:18). That is because, for him, the one flows, directly and necessarily, from the other. Love of neighbor arises out of love for God. He had taken and welded the two precepts into one.

In the Synoptic Gospels, only here and in Luke 11:42 is there word of human love of God, and it appears sparingly in the rest of the New Testament. Usually, the emphasis is on God's love for humankind. And this is as it should be. It is because God has first loved us that we love God (Rom 5:5,8; 1 John 4:11). And there is a test of the authenticity of our love of God: "Those who do not love a brother or sister whom they have seen, cannot love God whom they have not seen. The commandment we have from him is this: those who love God must love their brothers and sisters also"

(1 John 4:20–21). Jesus had shown in his life and death the quality of this twofold love. His love for God motivated his total dedication to his mission. His love for humankind marked him as one who had come to serve the saving purpose of God, one who had laid down his life as a ransom for humankind (Mark 10:45).

The scribe's reply (12:32–33) is proper to Mark: "You are right, Teacher; you have truly said that 'he is one, and beside him there is no other'; and 'to love him with all the heart, and with all the understanding, and with all the strength,' and 'to love one's neighbor as oneself'—this is much more important than all whole burnt offerings and sacrifices." He agrees fully with Jesus' answer and further specifies that the loving service of others is more important than elaborate cult. His insistence on love with the whole heart is a recognition that love cannot be measured. Love is incompatible with a legalism that sets limits, that specifies what one should do and should avoid. Jesus' assurance that this scribe is not far from the kingdom of God (12:34) is, in truth, an invitation. It is noteworthy that nowhere else in the Gospels does a scribe emerge in such a favorable light.

The Neighbor

In Luke's Gospel a scribe raised a related question, also disputed. "Who is my neighbor?" (Luke 10:29). The Essenes of Qumran, for instance, would maintain that all "sons of darkness," that, is, all who did not belong to the sect, should be excluded. Others, while less radical, would rule out "sinners." All would agree that, in the broadest interpretation, "neighbor" should be limited to Jews and proselytes. It is expected that Jesus, too, will respect the outer limits. It remains to be seen whether he will narrow them appreciably. The Good Samaritan (10:25–37) is his wholly unexpected answer.

Though not explicitly stated, it is certainly implied that the man who was mugged on the road to Jericho was a Jew (v. 30). His nationality is not expressly mentioned because the point of the parable is that the lawyer's question is not going to be answered in terms of nationality or race. Priest and Levite refused to become involved in what, one way or other, was sure to be a messy business (vv. 31 -33). Jesus did not accuse them of callousness; he did not pass judgment on their conduct. They were men who lacked the courage to love; dare we say they represent the common man? After priest and Levite it might have been expected that the third traveler—a series of three is typical of story—would turn out to be a Jewish layman; the bias would be anticlerical. The drama is that the third character, the hero of the story, was one of the despised Samaritans. He has been designedly chosen to bring out the unselfishness of love. The man applied first aid to the wounded traveler and carried him to an inn, and he did not consider that his obligations had thereby ended. Whatever a cynic might have thought of his conduct so far, the man turns out to be very much the realist. He did not naively presume on the softheartedness of the innkeeper but paid him, in advance, to look after the victim.

At the close, Jesus got the lawyer to answer his own question— "The one who showed him mercy" (v. 37). Yet, had he really responded to the original question? In verse 29 he had asked: "Who is my neighbor?" while the question that Jesus put to him in verse 36 is rather: "To whom am I neighbor?" The lawyer was concerned with the object of love and his question implied a limitation: My neighbor is one who belongs to such and such a group. Jesus looked to the subject of love: which of the three had acted as neighbor? The lawyer's question was not answered because it was a mistaken question. One cannot determine theoretically who one's neighbor is because love is not theory but practice. One's neighbor is any person who needs one's help, says the parable. The wounded man was neighbor to the priest and Levite just as much as he was to the Samaritan, but while they had theorized in the manner of the lawyer, he had acted. The traveler was neighbor to all three; the Samaritan alone was neighbor in return.

Though the recommendation of Jesus—"Go, and do likewise" (v. 37)—was addressed to the lawyer, it holds a message and a warning for all Christians. We may not pause to ask ourselves: "Is this person really my neighbor?" Christian charity knows no bounds. The pity is that there are so few "Samaritans" among us.

In respect of hope one may speak of human or historical hope and of fundamental or primordial hope. Historical hope has a particular human focus, for instance, hope of happiness in marriage. In contrast, fundamental hope is open-ended. While historical hopes may peter out in disappointment and frustration, fundamental hope enables people to overcome disappointment, to begin again, in hope. Indeed, the response of hope is part of being human—though there is the danger of despair: the death of hope.

The human person is a self-transcending being. The act of hope is an act of trust and of self-surrender. Hope arises from within the person, but in response to the broader world. Hope is animated by the stories of others. It is stimulated by challenge of "the not yet." If human hopes falter, fundamental hope, too, sooner or later, runs up against the limit-situations of human existence—the experiences of evil, suffering, death. It is then that it takes on a religious aspect as it affirms the existence and presence of a transcendent dimension to life itself. This does not necessarily mean that the object of hope is transferred to an other-worldly domain. Throughout most of the history of Israel the object of hope was firmly this-worldly. The location of biblical hope is within creation and history.

Christian Hope

Christian hope is founded on Jesus' preaching of the rule of God and of his praxis. The centerpiece of this hope is the paschal mystery of the death and resurrection of Christ. The risen Lord is, beforehand, the crucified Jesus. Christian hope resides in a historical reality including both darkness and light. It embraces both the present and the future, both this-world realities and other-world realities. We hope not only for eternal life but for justice, peace and integrity of life in this world. The ultimate purpose of God's plan for the world is not a glorified kingdom of disembodied spirits but rather a new heaven and a new earth. The Lord's Prayer makes clear that there is no heaven without earth: "Your will be done on earth as it is in heaven." The Christian God is the God of the cross, who stands in contrast to the detached Hellenistic God of omnipotence and impassibility. Dermot Lane pointedly asks: "Is the reality of an impassible God compatible with the revelation of God in Judaism and in the Cross of Jesus?" And answers: "I submit that the God revealed in the life and death of Jesus is analogically speaking 'a suffering God' and that the same God continues to suffer in the world until God comes again."[3] We shall see that biblical hope acknowledges, without remainder, the reality of suffering and makes no attempt to deny the inevitability of death.

Hope is not infrequently confused with optimism. They are markedly different. Optimism looks to human growth and progress. It tends to ignore the presence of so much evil and to play down the realities of pain and suffering. It fails to come to terms with human vulnerability. Hope acknowledges the ambiguity of human existence. It glimpses light in the midst of darkness. In the experience of suffering it asserts the possibility of healing. It insists on life in the face of death. It has been finely said of Christian hope: "In the end the Christian is someone who in the face of death goes into the garden of life with hope to plant a tree and knows that she will not plant in vain."[4]

The Old Testament

1. God

Faith

GRACIOUS CREATOR

*I*n Genesis 1 we learn that God, in whole freedom, set out to bring a universe into being, a creation with its own character and potential for development. A refrain—"God saw that it was good"—runs through the litany of creation, leading to the climactic declaration: "God saw everything that he had made, and indeed, it was very good" (Gen 1:31). Understandably for the time, the "world" of the narrative, ostensibly the universe, is, in practice, our world, planet Earth. "It is good": The Creator alone can say this of creation because the Creator alone can see the whole of it. We cannot look upon our world and say, with honesty, "It is very good." We cannot blind ourselves to so much that is, to our eyes, far from good. And we have been alerted to the danger of a one-sided reading of Genesis chapters 1 through 3—the reading of the text with almost exclusively anthropological focus. God has respect for the whole of creation. And this respectful God is not intrusive.

In the Genesis text "good" has the meaning of purposeful. But, what is this "purpose"? We need to look, more closely, at Creator and creation. This is just what Ruth Page has done.[5] Her finding is perceptive and challenging. She proposes a warm relationship between Creator and creation—a companionship. And she does point a way to a resolution of a perennial problem: reconciliation of gracious Creator and world of suffering. And not only human suffering, but the pain of all sentient creatures.

Possibility

God is God of freedom. God respects the freedom of creation through the gift of possibility. This sets up a relationship, based on

15

freedom, between God and creation. God works from no detailed blueprint. He lets possibility be. Multiple finite freedoms are set free to explore their own possibilities and make their own way. God respects the freedom of creation. God is God of love—and love does not manage the other. Evolution and history do not follow a divine script. The world is not determined, cast in a fixed, inflexible mold. Nor is it undetermined: without plan or pattern of any kind. Rather, it is determinable: It can bend to circumstances. Only such a world provides room for creaturely freedom.

This in no manner implies that God is an absentee Creator—one who created and then withdrew into Olympian aloofness. God is Creator in love with his creation. He is not "above" creation nor "in" creation—God is *with* his creation. To convey this, Ruth Page has coined the technical term "pansyntheism"—"God-*with*-everything." At one level this expresses the traditional notion that everything, at all times, stands in the divine presence. What is new in the emphasis is that this is no dominating presence but one that wholly respects and preserves creaturely freedom. It is a presence of companionship, a gracious, saving and forgiving presence. It follows that "if God accompanies *all* creation, there is no situation in either the human or the natural world without divine value, no situation in which human beings may act as if God were absent or uninvolved."[6] And, if God is "with" in this freedom-respecting manner, then the human creature has the freedom not to attend to this presence—and the freedom not to believe in its existence.

In no sense is pansyntheism denial of the transcendence of God or of his existence independently of creation. It does imply that God is never distant or aloof.

> [Pansyntheism] does deny that God's dwelling, the place where God is to be found, is only or partially a distant heaven....With pansyntheism there is no God observing from the centre to the outskirts that men and women are starving, homeless or oppressed, or that the planet is variously at risk. Rather, God is present with creation, in all that suffering as well as in its joy.[7]

Reference to suffering leads to a consideration of the natural—specifically, the animal—world. Those splendid animal-life television programs intrigue us. Animals fascinate us. But there is that disturbing food chain. If there are predators, there are victims. And the suffering of victims (warm-blooded creatures) is extremely disturbing. We have always had a problem with suffering in the human world (so much of it inflicted by humans). Animals follow their survival instincts. They must eat, and, to eat, carnivores have to kill—nature "red in tooth and claw." Is this how God planned creation? We have been so anthropocentric (human-centered) in our attitude to creation that we have ignored or depreciated the pain of other species. If, for us, suffering of innocent humans is a scandal and a challenge to any image of a loving God, must not the pain and suffering of other creatures raise even a bigger question mark?

In traditional theology, God is God of order. If this be so, the question looms larger. We then have to view all that suffering—and so much disorder—as a result of divine purpose, part of a divine plan. Belief in a loving God becomes an exercise in blind faith. But, if God is a God who allows possibility and respects freedom, if creation is free from God's shaping or directing hand, there is prospect of a more promising resolution. Pain and suffering are not of his devising. This is as true in the natural world as in the human. Turmoil in the natural world occurs not as feature of divinely devised aims but as a result of the free use of possibilities. God is present, but not responsible, when a lion brings down its prey or when a gunman slays his victim. The life of all creatures, including nonhuman creatures, is lived in the presence of God. This because God's freedom is not separate from God's love. Traditionally, there has been more stress on the almighty power of God than on his infinite love. It is true that God is almighty—but he does not "throw his weight about." He is God of might, indeed, but never God of force. When one reads the Bible aright, it is startlingly and comfortingly clear that he is, simply, God of Love. Though, ironically, the author of 1 John is singularly selective in his loving, he does hit the nail on the head when he declares, unequivocally: "God is love" (4:8).

Purpose

Because God created in freedom and is always with creation, there is inevitably a divine purpose in creation. How is that purpose achieved? It is achieved in moments where freedom and love become actual. In such moments concurrence with God takes place. Ruth Page makes an observation that is strikingly perceptive and theologically challenging:

> God is eternal, and wherever there has been concurrence with God, I believe that God's involvement in that moment makes it eternal as well....On the other hand, divine judgment is that, although relationship is always maintained with every creature, where there is no concurrence, or where there is no renunciation of consuming selfishness, there is nothing to harvest. These moments come under judgment, and fall into eternal oblivion.[8]

This makes sense—total sense. Good is always of God, and abides. Evil disappears into its own nothingness. This is reminiscent of Aquinas's insistence that evil is the absence of good: *malum est privatio boni.*

God's Need

God's creative deed is free. God had, absolutely, no need of the universe, no need of humankind. But he did bring us into being. As a result one can say, with truth, that humankind is necessary to God—necessary in the sense that a deed of God has to be meaningful. Creation was not a whim. God was in deadly earnest. There lies our hope, our assurance. God has made us for himself, has called us to be his children. God waits for our response. God needs us; needs us to know our need of him. A lesser God would have made a better job of it! He would have created beings who could not but acknowledge their dependence and be wholly thankful to their Creator. Our God has no time for slaves. His only weapon is love. His children will be freely his children — or not at all. Only a God who is God could call into being creatures who might dare to say no to their Creator.[9]

God is Creator of a universe. While we humans, with God's help, discern our place in his purpose, we have tended to be self-centered. Have we not been prone to see ourselves as, in some sort, focus of God's well-nigh exclusive attention? And, in our tiny corner of this vast world, we have acted, and do act, as though all else on our planet were solely for our use and benefit. We need a humbler view, a more realistic view. Humility is truth.

GOD OF FAITHFULNESS

In traditional theology, God is a changeless God. This alleged immutability of God may make some sense in a context of Greek metaphysics. It does not fit in a setting of biblical theology. The Yahweh of Israel, the *Abba* of Jesus, is not the Unmoved Mover of Aristotle but the God of Abraham and Moses. The God of our faith is not a Greek God but a Hebrew God, who is the *Abba* of our Lord Jesus Christ. Sadly, in our theology, that Greek God has prevailed. The Greek God is Olympian, remote, remorselessly logical, impassible, totally humorless and touchy about his divinity. The Hebrew God is exuberantly illogical, close at hand, can change his mind whenever he likes, suffers because of, with and for his people, and has little interest in covering his divine back. There is a *God!* The God of biblical revelation is not a God who stands aloof from creation. He is a passionate God, deeply in love with the work of his hands. And, throughout the Bible, is the refreshing anthropomorphism that keeps God real and near to us.

Apophatic theology—the *via negativa* (one can really only say what God is *not*)—is all very well. In its measure it is salutary, reminding us that we can never *know* the reality of God. But this surely not at the price of blunting biblical imagery. The writers of the Old Testament—poets many of them—were wholly sure that their God was God. Though they would not have recognized the term, their God was, emphatically, a *transcendent* God, but never an aloof God. Their conviction is summed up in a title favored by

Second Isaiah: the Holy One of Israel—a transcendent God, pre-occupied with his people. That is just the point. Our God is not a remote God. Our God is a God who feels and loves. If this is so of Israel's perception, what of the God who, through Jesus of Nazareth, has entered so fully into our history? In Jesus, "the reflection of God's glory and the exact imprint of God's very being" (Heb 1:3), we see the visage of our God. God is *Deus humanissimus*—the thoroughly human God. The genial paradox of Schillebeeckx is a definition of God which matches that implied by the *Abba* given to his God by Jesus.

Gracious Creator

God is *gracious* Creator. God is not mean-minded. Today, we have a perception, far beyond that of the biblical writers, of the well-nigh incredible grandeur of creation. We become more and more aware of the sheer vastness of the universe—a vastness that boggles the imagination. God has created with appropriately divine abandon. Our awe before the vast expanse of the universe leads to awe of the Creator. There is an even greater wonder. It is the assurance that this Almighty Creator, with a near infinite universe within his ken, has whole concern for humans on our puny planet: "What are human beings that you are mindful of them, mortals that you care for them?" (Ps 8:4). God has *divine* concern for us. This is not only our comfort—it is a measure of the true divinity of our God. The psalmist grasped and expressed the gracious magnanimity of the Creator when, in a tone of awe, he exclaimed of God's creation of humankind: "You have made them a little lower than God!" (8:5).

The God of the Bible, the Father of our Lord Jesus Christ, is the foolish God (see 1 Cor 1:18–21). His gamble was in making us free. He stands, stolidly, by that gamble. God is, happily, not an Unmoved Mover. God is not even Creator. God is *Parent*. And just there is the divine vulnerability. What loving parent can ever, ever reject the child? Our human grace is not that we are creatures of God, not even that we are image of God. The ultimate divine foolishness, made public in Christian revelation, is that we are *children* of God. That is Christian truth—but it must reach to all of humankind.

Response

There ought to be human response to God's love. Curiously, there is little explicit reference in the Old Testament (and even less in the New Testament) to humankind's love of God. Perhaps the response is presupposed. At any rate, in Deuteronomy the obligation is put with all desirable clarity:

> Hear, O Israel: the Lord is our God, the Lord alone. You shall love the Lord your God with all your heart, and with all your soul, and with all your might. (6:4-5)

This call to love became the opening words of the Shema ("hear"), the daily prayer of adult Jews. The context stresses what Yahweh had done for Israel; it underlines the fittingness of response. Because the divine love is total, the loving response must strive to be total. Halfhearted response points to something more serious than ingratitude. It is an admission that one has not yet known Love.

> So now, O Israel, what does the Lord your God require of you, but to fear the Lord your God, to walk in his ways, to love him, to serve the Lord your God with all your heart and with all your soul. (Deut 10:12)

Already we can catch the voice of the Johannine Jesus: "If you love me, you will keep my commandments" (John 14:15). God's love for us is not sentiment: It is active and efficacious love. Our response cannot be in words alone; it must be in service. And the service that God looks for is our service of one another. Response will have about it something of the quality of God's love. It will be outgoing and delicate, sensitive to others, giving them space to grow. Response is, too, in worship. If there is place for worship, there is greater place for service. Worship without service is sham—a point made vehemently by the prophets Amos, Hosea and Isaiah (e.g., Amos 4:4-5; 5:21-24; Hos 6:1-6; Isa 1:11; 29:13). One might add that worship should not be a display of pomp and circumstance. While there is place for solemnity, there is greater place for joy. And, always, an awareness of a God who is "not concerned with matters of consequence."

GOD OF SALVATION

We are conscious of struggle in our world. We experience struggle within itself. We imagine that God and evil are locked in combat. Nothing in our world would assure us that, in the last resort, good, not evil, will triumph. Faith in a benevolent Creator offers the only—and certain—assurance. The finitude of our existence is caught up in his world of creation. We are meant to be human beings in a sphere that is, simply, the world. It is futile to look for salvation beyond our creaturely existence. As Edward Schillebeeckx puts it:

> The world and the human history in which God wills to bring about salvation for men and women are the basis of the whole reality of salvation: there salvation is achieved in the first instance....In this sense it is true that there is no salvation, not even any religious salvation, outside the human world.[10]

Christian salvation is salvation of and for human beings—men and women of flesh and blood. The goal of salvation is the creation of a free society for free human beings. Salvation is not, nor was it ever meant to be, the salvation of "souls." It is a matter of healing, of making whole, the person. It includes and involves society and the world of nature. It comprises eschatological, social and political aspects. "Belief in God is a belief in God's absolute saving presence among men and women in their history....There is no situation in which God cannot be near to us and in which we cannot find him."[11] Salvation has been understood—or misunderstood—in so many ways. It surely cannot mean being shielded from our finitude and everything that this finitude involves. The process of salvation means that, here and now, we strive to be human—in our mortality and in our suffering. If this is not so, then Jesus of Nazareth is not the *whole* human being that our faith acknowledges him to be.

God and Sin

Throughout Genesis 6—9 (the flood story) we are in the presence of myth: an expression of universal truth in symbolic terms. It is a paradigm of an ongoing biblical concern. God represents infinite love and mercy and forgiveness. He wills the salvation of all. In fact, God would never launch a flood to destroy not only humankind but all earthly life. God is Creator, source and sustainer of life; he is not in the business of destruction. The Book of Wisdom puts it aptly: "All existing things are dear to you and you hate nothing that you have created—why else would you have made it?" (Wis 11:24). But...does that mean that God is unconcerned over sin and evil? Surely not. Here our limited understanding faces a daunting problem. How is one to portray the divinely loving forgiveness of God without conveying the false impression that he shrugs off sin as incidental? The beginning of an answer emerges when we understand that sin is not, and cannot be, a direct affront to God. Sin, whatever form it takes, is an affront to God's plan for his creation. Sin is betrayal of our humanness. Moreover, sin can be against our environment. Destruction of our world is sinful. We humans have sinned grievously against our animal cohabitants on this planet.

If we are to speak of God at all, we must speak in human terms. Unfortunately, we can begin to take our anthropomorphisms literally. We may tend to lose sight of the fact that God-language is always *analogical*. We can, and do, make statements about God that make sense to us. What is too often forgotten is that we cannot, and do not, know God *in himself*. I may say, with truth, that God is a loving God. I speak out of my experience of human love. Though I have not an inkling of the *reality* of divine love, my assertion is not meaningless. I may also speak of God as a just God. Again, my experience of justice is human justice: Let the punishment fit the crime. Here we begin to go hopelessly wrong. Our *just* God is reduced to our level. Accordingly, we have come up with a God who condemns sinners to hell—and rightly so! Objectively speaking, this is blasphemy. The error is that what reasonably operates as justice on the human level is taken to be operative in the world of God. Consider the following statement: God is a just

God who deals with us fairly. By human standards, impeccable. But...do any of us wish to be treated *fairly* by God? Do we wish our God to deal with us as we *truly* deserve? Surely, we hope to be treated with love and mercy. And that is how our just God does treat us—because divine justice *is* mercy.

We are left with the problem of evil and sin. We cannot accept that our God is unconcerned. There has to be a balance to the strange mercy of our God. So, there is the notion of the "wrath" of God. The idea of God oscillating between wrath and mercy is a misguided human attempt to find balance where, in divine terms, there is no balance to be struck. We ask the question: How may one reconcile God's mercy with God's justice? It is a mistaken question. The first Christian theologian got the matter right: "Has not God made foolish the wisdom of the world?...God's foolishness is wiser than human wisdom" (1 Cor 1:20,25). Too many later theologians misunderstood. Let us settle for a foolish God.

The comfort: This foolish God is determined to put up with his wayward children. Sadly, God would come to observe that the thoughts and inclinations of humans are perverse. Yet, he has determined that "never again shall there be a flood to destroy the earth." God will have the last word. He will because he is God of salvation and human salvation is all about becoming thoroughly human. And that means becoming truly child of God.

The Graciousness of God

Nothing escapes the eyes of God. How regularly this observation has been seen as sanction, as a threat. Jesus' perspective was quite other. "Your Father who sees in secret will reward you" (Matt 6:4,6,18). "Whoever gives even a cup of cold water to one of these little ones in the name of a disciple—truly I tell you, none of these will lose their reward" (10:42). God does indeed keep a close eye on us—but to acknowledge whatever good we do. Our good works carry no price tag; there is no "merit" in that sense. What is so much more important is "recompense": generous acknowledgment by a generous God. To God's eye, nothing of good we do is unobserved or unimportant. Not surprisingly because, wherever

24

there is good, it is of God. There are many, very many, who feel that they do not know God, yet, in fact, who witness to God — by doing good. They may not know God, but God knows them, and rejoices in them.

For one who claims to know God, it is vitally important that one knows or acknowledges the true God. When I have come to know, to experience, the graciousness of God, I will not only readily discern but firmly reject anything and everything that would temper or cloud this graciousness. This asks of me that I dare to acknowledge my God of infinite love and mercy and forgiveness.

In our world salvation is still a matter of hope. We may believe that, in principle, salvation has been achieved. Our experience, personal and of our world, constantly reminds us that, in practice, much is unredeemed. One listens to Paul: "We know that the whole creation has been groaning in labor pains until now; and not only creation, but we ourselves, who have the first fruits of the Spirit, groan inwardly while we wait for adoption, the redemption of our bodies. For in hope we were saved" (Rom 8:22 -27).

2. Humankind

Love

ur God is Creator. We are his creatures. There, already, is relationship. The quality of the relationship depends on the nature of the Creator. It could, conceivably, be a relationship of domination and subservience. That must be when God is regarded, wholly or primarily, as an authority figure. Where there is another, different, perception of God as loving and gracious, creaturehood will be assessed accordingly. And when God is perceived as a vulnerable God, there is a transformation. Now the relationship is one of Parent and child. God is still Creator, and very much God. God is a God who does not need slaves; God is a Parent who desires children. This is the God proclaimed by Jesus Christ, the God manifested in Jesus Christ. Here is a God perfectly recognizable in the Old Testament.

PARENT AND CHILD

In Genesis 1 the creation of humankind is written about with admirable directness and succinctness: "God created humankind [ha-adam] in his own image, in the image of God he created them; male and female he created them" (1:27). The Yahwist told the story in his manner (2:7-24). Yahweh molded a form out of dust from the earth. When he had breathed life into that form, behold a human being! Formed of dust from the ground, the human will return to the ground (a play on *adam* and *adamah,* "ground"); humankind is set, inexorably, on a course from birth to death. God made a home for *adam*—the man—and set a program for work: a trait and right of humanness. Yet, that *adam* is incomplete. "I will make him a helper as his partner"; "This at last is bone of my bone and flesh of my flesh" (2:18,23). The man now has a companion, a partner sharing life to the full. Now there is community and now there is whole humanity. "It is not good that the man should be alone." Human living cannot be understood only in relationship to God. Community, a harmonious relationship between men and women, is God's purpose for humankind. The community of man and woman is the basic shape of community.

Freedom

In the Genesis story, God issues a command: "You may freely eat of every tree of the garden; but of the tree of the knowledge of good and evil you shall not eat" (2:16-17). That command is an acknowledgment of human freedom. Humans can obey—or disobey. The temptation story (Gen 3) brings matters to a head. The function of the *nahash,* a talking snake—a stage prop—is to focus attention on the command (see Rom 7:9-11) and to spell out that disobedience is, in effect, a vain attempt "to be like God." It will remain the perennial human temptation. What is in question is, firmly, that God is God and humans are creatures. The simple fact is that the Creator cannot create God. What is created is, by definition, creature. We, as creatures, can achieve fulfillment *only in relation to* our Creator, not *without* him. Any human attempt to go it alone, to live without reference to God, is doomed to failure.

One realizes that sin is the deliberate rejection of a superior Power. It is an act of rebellion in which humans take the place of God and make themselves arbiters of morality and conduct. At the same time there is human effort and achievement that, if not taken with express reference to God, is not consciously in defiance of God. On the other hand, much is done and has been done in the name of God that he certainly does not condone. What it all boils down to in the end is that we, as creatures, can never break out of creaturehood. This is not because God is a jealous God—as the Genesis snake implied. He is a gracious God who will not settle for being no more than a benign Creator who looks kindly upon his creatures. God will settle for nothing less than Parenthood, with humans as beloved daughters and sons. Unhappily, the Cain and Abel story (Gen 4) shows that the brothers and sisters have not learned the human lesson too well. Society is meant to be people together in community. History, up to the present, is a sad tale of failure. Happily, our God is God of unyielding hope.

Parent

Nowadays it is not uncommon to find God referred to as Mother. The designation is not inappropriate. Because the Bible itself comes out of and reflects a patriarchal culture, it tends to be androcentric, male-centered. The predominant biblical metaphors for God are taken from male experience, with God being depicted as father, king, warrior and so on. At the same time, there is an intriguing openness to the use of female imagery with God being imaged as birth-giving woman and loving mother (see Deut 32:18; Isa 42:14; 66:13).

In point of fact it makes as much sense to refer to God as Mother as it does to call God Father. God is neither male nor female; God stands apart from such categories—God is transcendent. To call God Father is to acknowledge that God is the source of our being, of our life, in a manner that is, in some fashion, comparable to our parents' role: They conceive us and care for us. In that sense, God is Parent, but we do not *know* what divine "parenthood" might mean—except that it must outstrip infinitely, in graciousness, the most loving human parental relationship. It is due to linguistic convention (framed along patriarchal standards) that God is called Father and is spoken of in male terms. Feminist theology alerts us to the truth that the basic relationship is that of parent-child. The image of God, we are told in Genesis, is found in whole humanness: male and female together (Gen 1:27). Still, there is a pervasive view that God *is* male. Women have paid, and continue to pay, a high price for this manifestly mistaken perception.

Our God-language, including the God-language of Scripture, is emphatically male. Our God-image is andromorphic. The widely held corollary is that maleness reflects God in a way that female-ness cannot. If this were only theory, it would merely be silly. In practice, the attitude has sustained domination by men and the subordination of women not only in society at large but, tragically, in the churches too. Divine transcendence is compromised

28

when it is maintained that God is more appropriately represented as male rather than female.

Jesus addressed God as Father—indeed, more intimately, as *Abba*. He thereby expressed their relationship in the conventional language of his historical humanness. This tells us not only of his personal relationship with God but of the rich meaning of father-hood in his Hebrew tradition. This aspect has serious theological implications. But use of the title "Father," even by Jesus, does not mean that God is, in any sense, *male*. Appreciation of analogical language reminds us that we do not know what it means for God to be "Parent." It surely does not mean that God is male—or female for that matter. To wield the alleged maleness of God as a weapon of domination is perverse.

Children

God is a gracious Creator who loves his creation. God has cre-ated freely and with abandon. We need look no further than our own planet. The author of the Book of Wisdom wrote: "The great-ness and beauty of created things give us a corresponding idea of the Creator" (Wis 13:5). In creation, as we know it, humankind is God's masterpiece. God has put the earth in our care. God has, with divine magnanimity, made us free, challenging us to respon-sibility. God has, with divine graciousness, called us to be his chil-dren. What has been our response? Novelist Paul Gallico asks:

> Supposing God *had* made man, not in His own image, but in some reflection of His own love and spirit and turned him loose on earth to work out his own destiny. Must not His heart, must not any great creative, all-embracing heart be wrung with compassion for what His children had turned out to be?[12]

There is grief and sadness in the heart of God. There is no wrath, no anger. Only in our perversity do we imagine an angry God. After all, children, especially teenagers, tend to regard the care and concern of parents as oppressive. With regard to our Par-ent, we have been rebellious teenagers. With infinite patience God bears with us, not infringing on our freedom, but respecting our

29

dignity. God is saddened at seeing us enslave ourselves to other gods. Our Parent is saddened at the harm we have done: to ourselves, to others, to the whole of his earthly creation, grieved at the sheer burden of sin that weighs upon us. Our Parent is constantly calling out to us: "Here am I, here am I" (Isa 65:1). God waits for our response, waits not only in patience but with divine compassion.

The Son

The God who did not will to be alone has created humankind. From that human race, summoned forth in freedom, issued the one who responded, wholly. In him, the perfect response to God, God could be, God would be, God in history. God could, God now would, enter into human joy and human sorrow. God would have compassion with women and men in their pain and in their death. "God remembered Noah" (Gen 8:1): He would henceforth bear with humankind. "The Lord said to Abram" (12:1): He launched his plan to save humankind. "He did not spare his own Son" (Rom 8:32): God showed that he really is God *for us*.

Who, then, is God? Our God is Father of our Lord Jesus Christ who has shown himself in the life and cross of Jesus. God is truly the God of the Old Testament whom Jesus addressed as *Abba*. The difference is that, through the revelation of the Son, *we* see God more clearly. The New Testament brings more sharply and emphatically before us a concerned and caring Parent: "God so loved the world he gave his only Son" (John 3:16). God is the Father who has given us the Son—given us himself. We measure love by our experience of love. We have to measure even divine love by our human standard. To do so, however, we need to think the unthinkable, believe the unbelievable. God has revealed himself to us in the human person, in the life, death and resurrection of Jesus of Nazareth. In him God has come to walk with us. In him God has suffered among us and at our hands. He is always the same God, the one God, who speaks to us from the first page of the Bible to the last.

"[W]hat are human beings that you are mindful of them, mortals that you care for them?...You have made them a little lower than God" (Ps 8:4-5). The psalmist gazed on the broad sweep of the sky and across the Earth to the distant horizon. He looked at puny humans and wondered: "...you have made *them* little less than gods!" We realize that earth is but one planet in our galaxy, that it is an infinitesimally tiny speck in a vast universe. And we wonder that the Creator of the universe chooses not to be alone. There may be other creatures in other worlds with whom he has dialogue. We do not know. But we do know that God has called humankind into being, freely and of set purpose. Freely—because freedom is an essential attribute of God; freedom is of supreme value to our God. God has made us free and he meticulously respects our freedom. Often one hears the complaint: If God be God, why is our world in such a mess? Why does he not take steps to clean up the mess? The answer is, precisely, God's respect for human freedom. God might wave a magic wand. The cost is too high and he will not exact the price: the sacrifice of freedom. God might have programmed our world. But he does not choose to converse with robots. "Is the arm of the Lord shortened?" (Isa 50:2). The course of history might suggest that God has lost control of creation. The truth is, the verdict on creation—"God saw everything that he had made, and indeed, it was very good" (Gen 1:31)—is a verdict that God alone can pass. We glimpse but "the outskirts of his ways" (Job 26:134). God has had the first word. He will have the last.

Blessing and Task

Humankind receives a blessing: "...fill the world and subdue it, and have dominion" (Gen 1:28). The blessing sets up a special relationship between humans and their environment, and between them and the animal kingdom. "Dominion" carries heavy responsibility. The earth and everything in it and on it has been entrusted to humankind, but it remains God's property: "The earth is the Lord's and all that is in it" (Ps 24:1). God has concern for all of his creation, not only for humankind. Humankind has authority, but true authority calls for profound respect for the object of authority. It is of supreme importance that the blessing does not reach to the exercise of dominion over humans. God alone is Lord of humankind—humans are meant to be brothers and sisters. Jesus faithfully followed this pattern with his discipleship of equals and its paradoxical shape of authority—authority as *diakonia,* service. The domination that is hallmark of sin has no place in his scheme of things—"...it is not so among you" (Mark 10:42-45).

Humankind has a special task in our world. The transformation of the world, the development of a better and more tolerant human society, has been placed in the hands of contingent humans. We cannot expect God to relieve us of our responsibility and its consequent problems. We may not shift this back to God. It is our task to face up to and to strive with all the means at our disposal to overcome suffering and evil. It is our service, one that we perform in the presence of God. We shape our history, but we are not masters of it. God alone is Lord of history. We do our best within the limits of our finitude—and leave the rest to God.

Limits of Humanness

The notion that Genesis 2-3 has to do with an "original state," a state of original innocence forfeited by sin—thereby involving a "fall" into our present state—rests on a misunderstanding of the text. The story is concerned with human existence; it is not dealing with any historical situation. The "primal sin" is found in the fact that humans, in one fashion or another, do not want to acknowledge their own finitude. This is because finitude is regarded as a flaw rather than accepted for what it is: a necessary and inescapable feature of our creaturehood. It is human destiny to be human beings in a real world, a world that is wondrous but is also a world of failure and suffering. The finitude of the world and of humanity is not the result of a fall from grace. Our belief in God as Creator does not deny the finitude of creation, nor does it distort contingency into sin or fallenness. God abides with the contingent, that is to say, the world with its limitations and humankind in its finite humanity.

32

Humans are called to responsibility for their conduct: "Where are you?" (Gen 3:9). While humans cannot be made responsible for the origin of evil, humans remain answerable. The primeval story of Genesis looks to the human state as it exists in the lives of real men and women. The question there is: Why is the human being, created by God, limited by death, suffering, toil and sin? The question is not answered. The mystery of evil is left hanging—a mystery. The fact is that humankind is alienated from God—alienated but not cut off from God. Sin and death are part of human existence. Consciousness of nakedness had followed awareness of rebellion, awareness of guilt (3:7). God "clothed them" (3:21); the feeling of guilt is removed. God sent man and woman out into the world free of guilt feeling.

The Grief of God

The story of the Flood (Genesis 6–9) is of major theological significance. It dramatizes the destructive nature of sin and the reaction of God to sin. The episode of the "sons of God and daughters of men" (Gen 6:1–4) is meant to mark a stage, far beyond that of the man and woman of Genesis 3, in the futile human striving "to be like God." What is in question is wholesale corruption—to such a degree as to threaten human existence. God *has* to do something about the situation. Though his reaction is grief and sorrow, God unleashes the flood waters. Yet, the point of the story is: "God remembered Noah" (8:1). *Therein* is the turning point: From a path of destruction there is a turn to salvation—when God "remembers" things happen. The story ends in hope and promise: "I establish my covenant with you, that never again shall all flesh be cut off by the waters of a flood, and never again shall there be a flood to destroy the earth" (9:11). Even more significant is the repeated statement in the introduction and conclusion of the story. At the beginning "every inclination of the thoughts of their hearts was only evil continually" (6:5). At the close, after the promise that there will never be another flood, the similar observation is: "...for the inclination of the human heart is evil from youth" (8:21). God has decided to bear with humankind's tendency to evil.

Paradoxically, it is through perceiving the limitations of our world that we recognize the divinity of God. By the same token, it is how we come to evaluate the specific nature of humankind and of the world. Throughout the Bible the fundamental sin, one repeated throughout history, is to seek to abolish the limitations of creaturehood: to be "like God." The challenge, and the way of peace and salvation, is to welcome our creaturehood. "To enjoy and to love what is worldly in the world, is to enjoy and love what makes God God."[13] *Gloria Dei vivens homo*—God's glory lies in the happiness and well-being of humankind in our world, which is God's world. And God is with us in our finitude and in our involvement in this finite world. Our faith in God and our embracing of our humanness find apt expression in our prayer.

TALKING TO GOD

We might expect the Bible, as meeting place of God and humankind, of Parent and children, to have something to teach us about prayer. Prayer is one response to God, an intimate response. What may surprise us Christians is the naturalness of the prayer of Israel. Old Testament men and women spoke straightforwardly to their God. They turned to God with refreshing boldness. Theirs is no God of terror but a God who is personal and near. We have much to learn from that prayerful people.

Praise

Israel's God was a living God who offered life with dignity to his people. Praise was a natural response. The hymn acclaims God's redemptive deed as this continues among the people. It does not seek to make any return to God but joyfully acknowledges God's graciousness. The hymn of praise had its roots in the beginning of Israel's history, in recognition of the God who had acted in response to the people's cry of pain in Egypt. The song of Miriam (Exod 15:21)—inspiration of the later canticle of Moses

(15:1-19)—was a spontaneous celebration of the saving power of God. Hymns of praise achieved a new status in that encounter of God with his people, which is the liturgy as God is acclaimed not only for his deeds in the past but for his goodness here and now. Psalms of praise are notably present in the Psalter. And those that we term thanksgiving psalms are better regarded, also, as hymns of praise. It is worth noting that, when it comes to Old Testament prayer, many think exclusively of the Psalter. In fact, prayer pervades the Old Testament. Here one chooses to look not at praise but to other forms of prayer: lament and repentance.

Lament

We tend to be inhibited and formulistic in our prayer. We imagine that there is an appropriate manner of addressing God, a refined and courtly language befitting divinity. We expect God to conduct himself in a proper "godly" manner, and we assume that God expects us to be "proper" in our approach. We learn from the Old Testament that Israel, with a more robust understanding of God, could dare to complain to God of God, could talk back to him without restraint. An instance may alert us to this refreshing feature.

Moses was leader and mediator. When, however, he was sent to free his people, he found that his approach to Pharaoh served only to aggravate their plight. In exasperation he complained: "You have done nothing at all to deliver your people!" (Exod 5:23). Later, when the people had been delivered from Egyptian slavery, Moses learned, painfully, of human fickleness and of seeming divine unconcern. The people, scared by sudden freedom, yearned for security and turned on Moses and God. Moses was prepared to put his neck on the block. If Yahweh would not forgive the people's infidelity, then, "Blot me, I pray you, out of your book that you have written" (32:32). He reminded God that this unfaithful crowd left in his charge were *God's* people—*he* might try looking after them for a change (33:12-13)! Yahweh called his bluff. He proposed to destroy the rebels and make Moses father of a new people; Moses would have none of it (Num 14:13-19). Already we catch that comforting interplay. God has a sense of humor and watches our human posturing not with condescension but with gracious, if humorous, respect. He is a Parent who does not talk down to his children. Other striking examples of this startling, and comforting, dialogue are Jeremiah and Job.

LAMENT AS PRAYER

Creation faith accepts that God willed to create the world as it is and humans as they are. It accepts, without remainder, that finitude—contingency—is an inevitable feature of created reality. We are conscious of struggle in our world; we experience struggle within ourselves. The peril intrinsic to limitation and contingency is part and parcel of human existence. It is human destiny to be human beings in a world of failure and suffering. We live in a world that has more than its measure of pain. We need to come to terms with suffering as a factor of our experience—of life itself. Here is where lament comes in.

As not a few would see it, lament cannot be prayer; it can have no place in prayer. Suffering is to be borne: One "offers it up." This is not the view of the Bible. There, lamentation reflects the reality of human existence. If pain and suffering are characteristic of human existence (see Genesis 3), the expressing of pain is intrinsic to human life (see Mark 14:34-36; 15:34—Gethsemane and the cry on the cross). Lamentation is the language of suffering. Lament is addressed to God, because God is the One who can take away suffering. The language of suffering can be uninhibited in face of suffering that can no longer be comprehended. The accusation is mounted: How could God have allowed this to happen? The accusation is made in the context of talking with God, the context of prayer. It is the very relationship with God that makes the complaint possible. Think of the cross: My God, my God, why have you forsaken me?

LAMENT OF AFFLICTION

There are two kinds of lament of affliction: lament of the people—communal lament—and lament of the individual. Two questions recur in communal lament: "Why?" and "How long?" The question "Why?" asks why God had rejected, abandoned or forgotten his people. The question "How long?" implies enduring distress and expresses impatience at the duration. The point is that the accusatory questions are directed at God. Psalm 44 is a graphic illustration.

In this communal lament Israel ponders on the seeming absence of the God of Israel. It opens with a recital of God's interventions on behalf of the ancestors: "...our ancestors have told us what deeds you performed in their days, in the days of old (44:1-3). The victories of the Israelites were won by Yahweh's exploits on their behalf. Now, inexplicably, God has turned against his people: "...you have rejected us....You made us turn back from the foe....You have sold your people for a trifle....You have made us a byword among the nations" (44:9-16). The signs of God's dereliction of duty are glaring. To add insult to injury, God did not even demand a decent price for his property.[14]

Israel protests that it has not deserved such treatment:

All this has come upon us, yet we have not forgotten you,
or been false to your covenant.
Our heart has not turned back,
nor have our steps departed from your way. (vv. 17-18)

Worst of all, their God is responsible for the calamity:

Because of you we are being killed all day long,
and accounted as sheep for the slaughter. (v. 22)

This only sums up the emphasis throughout verses 9-16: God has to answer for the sorry situation. Then comes the bold challenge:

Rouse yourself! Why do you sleep, O Lord?
Why do you hide your face?

This is no time for God to sleep. It is high time God became conspicuous by his presence, not his absence. It is high time God remembers his covenant with his people. The psalm closes on this hope:

Rise up, come to our help
Redeem us for the sake of your steadfast love. (v. 26)

Here is robust prayer indeed. And it is only one instance. By itself it emphatically confounds a widespread delusion that the God of the Old Testament is a God who inspired fear—even dread. Instead, Israel had a refreshingly direct approach to its God—perhaps nowhere more than in prayer. While it is true that most of the communal psalms do acknowledge the people's sin, always the ultimate hope is in Yahweh's covenant faithfulness.

As for the individual lament, Psalm 88, the core of it at least, is a mind-boggling cry to God that boils down to unmitigated accusation of God. Here is one who has had a wholly unhappy life ("from my youth," v. 15). He has had enough and cries out to God. The startling factor is the accusing "you." All his misery is laid at the door of God. *You* have caused all my sufferings, *you* have turned my friends against me, *your* fury rains upon me (vv. 6-8, 16-18). I have prayed to you—you don't listen (vv. 9, 13-14)! The implication: Get your act together, God; I have had it! Only—this is a cry of faith. What we learn is that God is not happy with sycophants. God may not be too comfortable with the righteous. But he exults in those who take him seriously enough to fight with him.

Repentance

For the people of Israel lament was a powerful way of prayer. It was a firm part of their tradition and, because of the prominence of lament in the Psalter, it was an abiding feature of their worship. There is, however, a different manner of talking to God. It is one thing to challenge God from the ground of striving to do his will. But when one is conscious of having failed, and failed dismally, what does one do? In this situation we find that postexilic prayers (prayers in the aftermath of the sixth-century Babylonian Exile) are encouragement and comfort. These prayers are straightforward: We have sinned; we deserve all that has come upon us. Are we depressed? No! We have sinned, we have failed—but you are *you.* It is, in some sort, an anticipation of: "I shall arise and go to my Father."

Trauma of Exile

What was a native of Judah to think when God's covenant with Abraham (Gen 17:6-7) and his solemn promise to David (2 Sam 7) had come to nothing? There was no questioning the harsh reality of Nabuchadnezzar's conquest: temple, city and nation were gone. On the strength of Yahweh's word it ought not to have been so, but it had happened. For the thoughtful Yahwist the disaster was a mirror held up to the nation, a mirror that reflected a visage of gross failure and sin. Some, at least, had learned from the bitter experience of the Babylonian Exile: The faith answer to the disaster was repentance and hope. The people had failed—of that there could be no doubt. But Yahweh was steadfast as ever. There was a way of restoration, a way of redemption. It was the way of candid confession of sin and of total trust in God's boundless mercy. The many moving postexilic prayers to be found in Baruch, Ezra-Nehemiah, Tobit, Sirach, Esther, Judith and Daniel firmly follow this way.[15]

While postexilic prayers tend to be lengthy, there is about them a refreshing candor and an inspiring faith. They are the prayers of a chastened people, a people that, in adversity, had found its soul. These who pray confess sin openly. They do not grovel but maintain a quiet dignity. Prayer should always be worthy of the God who is addressed and of the people of God who pray. Most instructive is the recurring phrase that characterizes God as "the great and awesome God who keeps covenant and steadfast love with those who love him and keep his commandments"—followed always by the confession: "We have sinned." These later Israelites had come to understand that the "awesome God" is such only to those who have never known him. Those who pray these prayers have discovered the way of restoration, the way of redemption.

The God Who Grieves

We live in a world that has more than its measure of pain. Israel did not suffer stoically but cried out to a God who could relieve pain. Here is a lesson we Christians could profitably take to heart.[16] We live in a world of sin; we are sinners among sinners. Again, Israel points the way of candid confession of sin and of total trust in God's boundless mercy. Lament and repentance: there is no conflict. I can know that I am a sinner. It may well be that my sufferings are due to my frailty. I must be sure that they are never sanctions imposed by a judgmental God. This, of course, runs counter to the current view of Israel, illustrated in these prayers of repentance, that personal and national disasters were divine punishment.

There has been the human tendency to picture God as offended, angered even, by human sin. The truth is: Sin, whatever form it takes, is an affront to God's plan for his creation. And God, the Creator, *grieves* over sin. There is grief, and sadness and suffering in the heart of God. There is no wrath, no anger. With infinite patience God bears with us, not infringing on the freedom with which he has endowed us, but respecting our dignity. He is grieved at the sheer burden of sin that weighs upon us. God is constantly calling out to us: "Here am I, here am I" (Isa 65:1). He waits for our response, waits not only in patience but with divine compassion. I come before my God as sinner. I approach, humbly, but with a dignity that becomes God and me. And, sinner though I am, I can cry out at the unfairness of suffering.

We are children of God: *sinful children*. We have not responded fittingly to his goodness; we have taken advantage of his love. We are sorry, or ought to be, for our failures. But our God does not want us to feel guilt. God is a God of compassion who is with us in our sorrow. God is a God of forgiveness, and his forgiveness is prompt and total. We, then, should have the decency—the humility—to acknowledge our failures: "God, be merciful to me, a sinner."

3. Vision of Hope

Hope

 t might be argued that our theological portrait of God veils rather than reveals the true God. We do issue warnings on the hazards of God-language, on the need for realizing that it is always analogical: that anything we can say of God falls very short of the mark. It seems that we regularly ignore the warnings. We end up with a superficially neat God who does not recognize himself in our portrait of him. It may be that our only hope of reflecting anything of God is in the language of poetry. We might listen to the genial poet-author of Job. He had sketched the might and wonder of the Creator (Job 26:5-13) and then ruefully observed:

> Lo, these are but the outskirts of his ways;
> and how small a whisper do we hear of him! (26:14)

WORD OF HOPE—THE PROPHETS

When one looks closely at the text of the prophetical books, one observes a striking and consistent factor. Not alone in the juxtaposition of oracles but, regularly, within an oracle, we find an abrupt change of mood. There is warning and threat, usually extensive, to a stubborn and unfaithful people. Then, out of the blue, comes word of salvation. There is no logic to it. That is the beauty of it, and the comfort. There can be no logic because salvation is sheerly grace. God, we have already observed, is exuberantly illogical. God's word always is forgiveness. It has to be. God, freely, took the risk of creating humans as free beings. God must, consequently, take responsibility and pay the price. His divine generosity in creation must be matched by the divine generosity of his mercy. A prophetic Paul had glimpsed that. When, at the close of Romans 9-11, he had bidden goodbye to logic, he could declare not only, "All Israel will be saved" but also, "For God has imprisoned all in disobedience so that he may be merciful to all" (Rom 11:26,32). The prophet Paul is here in the line of the prophets of Israel. And, of course, in line with the prophet Jesus.[17]

The Prophets

Why is it that the prophets have achieved and sustained such influence? It is, in large measure, surely, because of the power of their language. It is not by chance that the prophets, all of them, were poets. The God imaged by them is presented in words that match their poetic insight. In painting divine emotion they play on the gamut of human emotions. And, with poetic abandon, they can present contradictory pictures of God: a God who will not hesitate to punish sinners; a God who has preferential option for sinners. The biblical God is anything but the immutable, impassible God of our theological tradition. He, along the line of prophetic understanding, is a full-blooded, indeed an earthy God. And never for a moment is he any other than God.

People of their day, the prophets took divine causality very seriously. Theirs was the common assessment voiced in Job: "Shall we receive the good at the hand of God, and not receive the bad?" (Job 2:10). Again, they went along with the doctrine of retribution: God rewards virtue and punishes sin. Since, by and large, the prophets had to contend with national disasters—or the threat of them—it was natural for them to view such disasters not only as due to the sinfulness of the people but, also, as divine punishment of sin. It is not surprising that oracles of woe predominate. It is an aspect of their keen pastoral concern.

Grieving God

Like anthropomorphism, the attribution of human features and behavior to God, anthropopathism (the attribution of human emotions to God) is common in biblical language. Anthropopathism must point to the *pathos* of God. The Greek word refers to what one has experienced; it surely includes experience of suffering. If we are to be true to the whole biblical picture, we shall need to pay far more attention than we have had to metaphors that point to the suffering of God.[18] Neglect of them has contributed, in its measure, to a prevailing image of God as a Dominating Being. Neglect of them has caused many to turn away, in disgust, from a God who appears to display disdainful unconcern for human suffering. Most importantly, these metaphors of pathos are essential ingredients of a balanced portrait of God. They add, immeasurably, to God's attractiveness and counter, effectively, many false gods of our religious heritage.

There is, surely, something compelling about a God who grieves for humankind gone astray. A God who suffers because of the people's rejection, who suffers with his suffering people, who suffers on behalf of the people, is, indeed, a challenging God—the foolish God discerned by Paul. This is the God who has shown that he is a God not aloof from pain and sorrow and death. This is the God of humankind. This is the *kind* of God we need. This is *our* God.[19]

Our traditional ideas of God may cause us to be somewhat upset by biblical language. It is all very well to hear of the "love" of God. What of God's "wrath"? In the first place it is needful to observe again that human language is incapable of enunciating the ineffable reality of God. It, however, remains our only tool. Biblical language reminds us that God is not some vague "force"; God is personal. The language reflects a vitally important perception. The prophets and biblical writers were conscious of the transcendence of Yahweh. They were intensely aware that he was a God close at hand, a God with whom they could and did have dialogue. In speaking of God and to God they were prepared to take risks.

HOSEA

A striking case in point is Hosea. He was the first to represent the covenant relationship of Yahweh with his people as a marriage. It would have seemed natural enough that the covenant between God and Israel might have been likened to the marriage contract. In practice, it is not the contract aspect that is exploited but, instead, the love aspect, and especially the love of a husband for his wife. Hosea harked back to the wilderness and the entry into the land. He looked to the graciousness of God and the rank ingratitude of Israel (Hos 9:10; 11:1-12; 13:4-6). Doubtless, Hosea idealized the wilderness years and painted them as the honeymoon period of God and his people. What matters is that he did not hesitate to cast Yahweh as Spouse of Israel. Bold imagery indeed when the Canaanite religion of Baal was the great challenge: the fertility cult of Baal and his consort Astarte. The prophet knew that, despite the risk of confusion, what mattered was to proclaim the love of God. Theological prudence would not deter him from flaunting his profound conviction. Some might misunderstand—too bad. But those who, like himself, had known the joy and the pain of love would recognize in his long-suffering Spouse their one, true God.

It is plain that the prophets who had, pastorally, to face intransigence from political and religious leaders and from their own people retained an insight into divine mercy. Beyond their warnings there is ever a perception of the profligacy of God. He just will not be confined. God's last word simply has to be word of forgiveness.

AMOS

Amos is the exception that proves the rule. He is a prophet of unrelieved gloom. On the other hand, the present shape of the book of Amos firmly sustains our argument. The final editor felt compelled to provide a thoroughly optimistic conclusion. Nothing up to Amos 9:10 would lead us to expect 9:11-15.

> On that day I will raise up the booth of David that is fallen....
> I will restore the fortunes of my people Israel....
> I will plant them upon their land,
> and they shall never again be plucked up
> out of the land that I have given them,
> says the Lord your God. (9:11,14,15)

There is no human logic: the oracle is wholly out of tune. Instead there is a divine logic. It is dramatic expression of God's final word—word of salvation. The prophets bear abundant witness to divine illogicality.

THEREFORE...

The prophet Hosea bears startling witness.

Plead with your mother, plead—
for she is not my wife, and I am not her husband....
Therefore I will hedge up her way with thorns;
and I will build a wall against her,
so that she cannot find her paths....
Therefore I will take back my grain in its time....
I will punish her for the festival days of the Baals,
when she offered incense to them...
and went after her lovers,
and forgot me, says the Lord. (Hos 2:2,6,9,13 [italics added])

In verses 6 and 9 the "therefore" (*laken*) introduces, as generally in prophetic texts, a threat (see Amos 3:2; Mic 3:12; Hosea 4:3). The next "therefore" (v. 14) strikes a surprisingly different note.

Therefore I will now allure her,
and bring her into the wilderness,
and speak tenderly to her....
There she shall respond as in the days of her youth,
as at the time when she came out of the land of Egypt....
And I will take you for my wife in righteousness and in justice, in steadfast love and in mercy. I will take you for my wife in faithfulness, and you shall know the LORD. (2:14-15, 19-20)

In verse 14 "the 'therefore' of intense judgment has been transposed into an act of protection and solidarity....The voice of harsh threat has inexplicably become the sound of *assurance*."[20]

In sorrow, Yahweh had divorced his spouse: "...she is not my wife and I am not her husband." Here, as at Babel where God's will to scatter humankind out of his sight (Gen 11:1-9) faltered on the call of Abraham to a new beginning (12:1-3), and as at the Flood when the grim decision, "I will blot out from the earth the human beings that I have created...for I am sorry that I have made them," flows directly into the declaration, "But Noah found favor in the sight of the Lord" (6:7-8), God is inconsistent. Ever, God's weak side is his love. Divorced Israel may be:

45

the price of unfaithfulness. In God's eyes Israel is still his spouse and he will not give her up.

One might document, throughout the Old Testament prophets, a remarkably consistent pattern—indeed, one has done so.[21] It is a pattern of abrupt contrast between divine word of threat and condemnation and a following word of forgiveness and salvation. Not infrequently—and this is especially so in Second Isaiah (Isa 40–55)—the message of consolation stands by itself, without immediate negative contrast. Elsewhere, the fluctuation can be noted over and over again. It is not a rarity; it is the norm. It offers a firm pointer. God's last word is forgiveness and salvation. And this feature is to be found not only in the prophets. The God of the Bible, the Father of our Lord Jesus Christ, is the foolish God (see 1 Cor 1:18–21). God's gamble was in making us free. He stands, stolidly, by the gamble. God is, happily, not an Unmoved Mover. He is not even Creator. God is PARENT. And just there is his divine vulnerability. What loving parent can ever, ever reject the child? Our human grace is not that we are creatures of God, not even that we are image of God. The ultimate divine foolishness, made public in Christian revelation, is that we are *children* of God. That is Christian truth—but it must reach into all of humankind.

CHALLENGE TO HOPE—JOB

The Riddle of Suffering

There are experiences common to all human beings such as the experience of birth and death—and the experience of suffering. We humans are so fragile, so vulnerable. We are so open to disease that may touch us even before birth. Pain and suffering, to a lesser or greater extent, are part of our human lot. But let us be honest about it. A frightening share of human suffering is wrought by humans. Man's inhumanity to man is the great sin, the challenge to God's loving purpose for his children. I have used *man* in a generic sense. Taken in a gender sense, man's inhumanity to woman, rampant in many cultures and serious in ours, is obscene perversion of God's purpose. We bring much pain upon ourselves and upon others.

There remains the suffering that is not of our causing. Herein lie both riddle and scandal. Suffering that has a human source we can understand—though we still ask: Why? Suffering that seems to come, in some fashion, from our God—that is profoundly disturbing. Must our suffering be ascribed to an allegedly beneficent God? Early Israel could simply answer: Yes, God is author of suffering. Later Israel modified this view. The Christian must repudiate it. But, then, the problem of innocent suffering becomes more, not less, acute. It is not a new problem. It is obvious that the first Christians were embarrassed by the suffering and death of Jesus—the Messiah. They solved the problem in terms of enigmatic divine purpose: "...this man, handed over to you according to the definite plan and foreknowledge of God, you crucified and killed" (Acts 2:23).

We should be clear, however, that the "definite plan and foreknowledge of God" does not envisage an inflexible divine strategy. It is, in fact, a manner of saying: *We* do not know why the Son, the sinless one, had to suffer and to die. *God* knows. Jesus laid down his life in loving response to the Father's love—love of the Son and of humankind. The Father did not demand the death of Jesus. The Father did not seek the death of Jesus: "Surely they will respect my Son" (Mark 12:6 and parallel texts). The Father gave his Son for humankind—and gave him *eis telos,* in boundless love. God would show human beings that his love for them was in deadly earnest. The Father did not bring about the death of the Son—Jesus died at the hands of his religious and political enemies. But the Father did not shrink from having him "delivered up" to his enemies. Only so does the death of Jesus fall within the "definite plan and foreknowledge of God." And, in filial acceptance of God's saving purpose, and only so, did Jesus accept death. He was obedient unto death—with an obedience that was a loving yes to a purpose of sheerest love. "God so loved the world...." There is no gainsaying that word. It is the only explanation of the death of Jesus that is consonant with the character of our God.

As regards innocent suffering in general, the answer lies in faith. We Christians must emulate the faith of the mighty Job who, when faced with the arbitrariness of his God, clung to his faith in the merciful God of his previous experience. Faith does not call for a suspension of reason. It assures us, instead, that God is greater than our reasoning. Unmerited suffering, innocent suffering—that is wrong, that is scandal. Our God is not unmindful of the scandal. His Son, the sinless one, suffered. We Christians must leave the mystery of suffering in the hands of God, trusting that his love has the answer to the perennial riddle. This is not to say that we do not strive to understand it as best we may. At least we can unburden ourselves of misunderstanding. And we have the right to lament, to cry out to God, the right to ask "Why?" and "How long?"

Job

Israel tended to explain the suffering of the nation as being the result of God's anger at the sinfulness of his people. In time the dominant view was that suffering always had its source in sin—in hidden sin it may be. There can be no innocent suffering. This was the orthodox position maintained by Job's "comforters"—his theologian friends. To balance it, stress was laid on God's willingness to forgive: He takes no pleasure in human suffering, in any suffering. Where there is repentance he will restore to life—to union with himself (see Ezek 18).

The author of Job was a theologian-poet of imposing stature, a man of sterling literary skill and of devastating faith. He found his plot in a story about a legendary Edomite sheik who, when tested by Satan—not yet the evil spirit of later tradition—proved unshakably faithful. The author faced up with merciless candor to the problem of suffering and, with delightful verve, assaulted orthodox theology. He dared to set experience against theory. Of course the theory, well entrenched, shrugged off his arrows, and went its unrealistic way. But, when Jesus came, he sided with Job against the orthodox.

The person who cries out in pain over suffering has a dignity of his own which neither men nor gods can rob him of. The story of Job makes this evident; and since that time no theology can fall below Job's level. The theology of "Job's friends" is confuted. Does Job have any real theological friend except the crucified Jesus on Golgatha?[22]

The prose sections, Job 1:1-2:13; 42:7-14, though surely rewritten by the author, do reflect the original story. And that story, naive as it may seem, is an essential part of the work. As a matter of fact, it is vitally important for an understanding of Job. Job protested his innocence while his friends were convinced of his guilt. Who was in the right, they or he? Without the prologue (1:1-2:13) we would have no means of knowing. But this prologue puts the reader in the picture. The trials of Job follow on a wager between God and Satan. Twice (1:8; 2:3) God acknowledged the righteousness of "my servant Job"; twice Job's steadfastness is asserted (1:22; 2:10). And the epilogue (42:7-14), with its description of the restoration of Job's fortunes, is a vindication of his righteousness. The reader is left in no doubt. (Job and his friends remain in the dark.) The cynical Satan renders a further service. His question, "Does Job fear God for nothing?" (1:9), strikes to the heart of the work. The implication is that Job was "blameless and upright" because it was well worth his while to be so. The issue is: Can there be disinterested service of God? Can one cling, in faith, to God when the clinging seems pointless? Is God, and God alone, enough? Job's response is firmly affirmative. And God's trust in his servant was wholly vindicated.

> God trusts his servant—trusts him with the maintenance of eternal truths, trusts him to stand by them to the last. The trust is itself a reward, the reward of innocence, and the confirmation of piety, as much an honour as the sufferings of Plato's just man crucified. We often speak of trusting God; is there not a neglected truth in the thought that God is trusting us?[23]

The sturdy faith of Job is, indeed, thought provoking. Can a human serve God for the sake of God—and for no other reason? That "service" is saying yes to God in face of total contradiction. It is letting God have the last word.

In the dialogues (chapters 3-31) Job wrestled with a tormenting problem: He suffered, yet knew himself to be innocent. The inadequacy of the traditional view (the traditional doctrine of retribution, in its simplest form, is that the good are rewarded and the wicked are punished in this life) has become apparent, but people can close their eyes to a disturbing new truth. *In this life:* At the age of the Book of Job, in Israel, there was yet no concept of life after death. That came only in the second century B.C.

Here the three friends (Eliphaz, Bildad and Zophar) are the champions of "orthodoxy." They had accepted the classic teaching without question and quite refused to admit that it will not fit the facts of the present case. Their position was stark: Suffering is punishment of sin; if one suffers, it is because one is a sinner. The facts must be made to fit the theory! Hence they proceeded to comfort the sufferer by insisting that he must be a sinner, and they grew more insistent as he protested his innocence. To Job himself the inadequacy of the traditional theology was painfully obvious.

NEVERTHELESS...

Job's theological problem ran deeper: he was faced with the arbitrariness of God. He, a righteous one, had been stripped of every reward of his virtue and was being treated as a gross sinner. It made no sense. Up to now, in the days of his prosperity (see chapter 29), he had gone along with the theological view that suffering is always consequence of sin. It seemed eminently reasonable. After all (the other side of the coin) his own prosperity was seal on his righteousness. Now, that comforting theology—comforting if one is on the "right" side—had failed him. He is sufferer; and he knows himself to be innocent. The theologians of orthodoxy—for whom there was no scope for "dissent"—would persuade him to compromise his integrity: to plead guilty when he knows he is not guilty.

> Job was justified in holding to his innocence; suffering is no proof of sin. If that has become to us a commonplace, let us learn from such a book as this what it sometimes costs to reach a commonplace, before it has become common.[24]

The alternative was to admit that God was arbitrary and unjust. He was trapped. The author has brilliantly sustained the contrast between two irreconcilable theological stances. Indeed, he has shown how Job and his friends drift further apart. And, perhaps not without a little malice, he shows that while they become more and more sure of themselves, Job becomes more and more open to God.

50

The Book of Job is, and always will be, a radical challenge to any theology that seeks to operate outside of experience. Indeed, the author has brilliantly devastated any *neat* theological system. The three theologians had seen themselves as champions of God, defending his cause against the "heretic" Job. At the close there is the shock: "My wrath is kindled against you...for you have not spoken of me what is right, as my servant Job has" (Job 42:7). The author twists the knife as he has the orthodox theologians forgiven by God at the intercession of the heretic (42:8-9). They had pushed the cause of their God, a theoretical God. And Job rebelled: He sought the true God. The Book of Job is the biblical charter of theological "dissenters."

THE ABSENCE OF GOD

More agonizing still for Job than his attempt to cope with the problems of retribution and of innocent suffering was his sense of the absence of God. Job kept crying out to a God who would not answer. His experience is a classic instance of the "dark night of the soul" described by later mystics. God had not withdrawn—but Job had felt that he had. In reality he was, in his groping, growing closer all the time to that hidden God. He had shouted out, in pain and frustration, to a God who will not answer. Yet, his God cannot, surely, be callously deaf to Job. Job's sturdy faith will not allow it to be so:

> If I go forward, he is not there;
> or backward, I cannot perceive him;
> on the left he hides and I cannot behold him;
> I turn to the right but I cannot see him.
> But he knows the way that I take;
> when he has tested me I shall come out like gold. (23:8-10)

In his frustration and anger, Job yet came to glimpse the God veiled from the eyes of his theologically complacent friends. With wonder he recognized that God can be wholly preoccupied with one suffering human. He learned that the seemingly aloof and silent God was a God who willed to be within the human world. He chose to be present to the finitude and frailty of a powerless and afflicted human being. He is the God who is present to and in human suffering.

Job won through by faith—and what a robust faith. He dared to speak out to his God, dared to warn his God. If God had, as it seemed, grown tired of Job and would abandon him to death, he might think again. After all, it is he who will be loser—he will have one worshiper less!

> For now I shall lie in the earth;
> you will seek me, but I shall not be. (7:21)

Job knew that God wants humans to be human; he does not ask us to grovel. He was clear that our status is God-given. H. W. Robinson contrasts Job with Prometheus:

> Prometheus, chained to his rock for bringing divine gifts to men, defies Zeus to do his worst; in that defiance we have the Greek spirit of restless energy. But Job, on his dung-heap, torn not by an eagle but by leprosy, defies the sufferings which almost overwhelm him to rob him of his faith in a hidden God; in that faith you have the great Hebrew contribution to human history.[25]

There is the grandeur of Job.

Job had, throughout, stoutly proclaimed his righteousness. He had, early, turned from the theological rectitude of his "friends." He challenged God: a painfully absent God, a wholly silent God. Yet, he had no final resort except in this God. In chapter 31 he took the ultimate step: his oath of innocence. It reflects accepted legal procedure. When an accused person knew oneself to be innocent but could not prove it or summon witnesses to sustain it, one threw oneself on the mercy of God. The idea is: May God strike me dead if my protest is not true. A weary Job took this desperate step. At the close it is firmly stated: "The words of Job are ended" (31:40). He had catalogued, in detail, his unblemished righteousness. And at the end he dared to throw down the gauntlet to the adversary—this perverse, silent God, this strange God who is still the God of his faith and trust:

Oh, that I had one to hear me!
Oh, that I had the indictment written by my adversary!
Surely I would carry it on my shoulder;
I would bind it on me like a crown;
I would give him an account of all my steps;
like a prince I would approach him. (31:35-37)

One closes with a fittingly splendid comment:

> Prince-like—we cannot leave Job with any truer word than that. He
> has been princely in his despair as well as in his hope. He has won
> the victory of faith over the world, the flesh and the devil. He has
> refused the suggestion to doubt his own conviction of innocence;
> he has conquered the temptation to conceive God as ultimately
> unjust, to which for a time he yielded. The problem of Job on its
> theoretical side is as obscure as ever to him; he is quite unable to
> account for the union of suffering and innocence in his own case,
> and, as he has come to think, in the case of many others. But he
> has solved it as a practical problem; he has won through man's the-
> ories about God to God himself. Like Hosea, he sees God's love to
> be deeper than God's wrath. His challenge is really a prayer, and
> prayer, as a great scholar has rightly said, is the only adequate
> expression of faith.[26]

CHALLENGE OF HOPE—JONAH

"... something greater than Jonah is here." (Matt 12:41)

The Babylonian Exile of 587 B.C. was traumatic in the extreme for
Israel—more precisely, for Judah. One can get some measure of it in
the warnings, and the manifest pain, of Jeremiah and Ezekiel.
Thanks, in great measure, to the exuberant hope and vision of Second Isaiah (Isa 55-66) there was a restoration. It was a return from
exile on a pitifully small scale. Restoration was slow and painful, a
fact graphically documented in Ezra and Nehemiah. The new Judah
was a tiny territory. Understandably, a defensive ghetto mentality
prevailed. It was a case of "we" and "them." *They*, all others, were the
enemy. But God is on our side. God is, exclusively, our God.

One, at least, in Judah had a broader vision. He stood in the
line of Second Isaiah, a prophet who had designated Cyrus the

Persian a "Messiah"—a pagan king "anointed" to deliver God's people (Isa 45:1).

> I have aroused Cyrus in righteousness,
> and I will make all his paths straight;
> he shall build my city and set my exiles free. (45:13)

Cyrus, in overcoming the Babylonians, had served God's purpose. The author of Jonah, worthy heir of Second Isaiah, had discerned an implication of that prophet's view of the providential role of Cyrus. He gave voice to his insight in a brilliant satire.

Reluctant Prophet

It is sad that, for long, this little writing was grossly misunderstood and its message quite missed. The fine point of that message is startling, as we shall see. The author had discovered a convenient hero, a biblical prophet who was a name—nothing more: "Jonah son of Amittai" (2 Kgs 14:25). He was free to make of this Jonah what he would. He made the most of his opportunity.

"The word of the Lord came to Jonah" (Jonah 1:1): He was, unmistakably, a prophet. His mission was seemingly in the line of traditional prophetic concern: "Go at once to Nineveh, that great city, and cry out against it; for their wickedness has come up before me" (1:2). While there had been prophetic oracles against pagan nations and cities, the difference here is that a prophet is sent with a message of warning *to* a pagan city. Moreover, that warning is for "Nineveh, that great city," capital of Assyria. In Israel, Assyria had long been a symbol of oppression; it had become the "great Satan." The prophet Nahum had gloated over its fall (in 612 B.C.). An aged Tobias could die a happy man: "...before he died he rejoiced over Nineveh, and he blessed the Lord for ever and ever" (Tob 14:15). Against this background it is, after all, not so surprising that Jonah "set out to flee to Tarshish from the presence of the Lord" (Jonah 1:3). Commanded to go east, toward modern Iraq, he hastened to take ship for Gibraltar.

As prophet, he ought surely have known better: One does not so easily escape the Lord. Jonah's ship of flight sailed into a mighty tempest. The divinely provoked storm was not an expression of divine anger; it was the start of God's playful coping with his reluctant prophet. For the author, Jonah personified the narrow outlook he pilloried. Jonah stood in sharp contrast to the other characters of the story—all of them responsive and generous (and pagan!).

The fierce storm was never meant to be ultimately destructive. The story's characters were not aware of this. While the scared sailors frantically sought to save their ship, Jonah slept, calmly, in the hold. A peeved captain shook him awake and bade him pray to his god. It was obvious that an impious one had occasioned the violent storm: A god was surely angry. Lots were cast to uncover the culprit. Jonah stood guilty. The pagans were aghast at his crime: He had dared to disobey a firm command of his god! Jonah assured the crew that they could save themselves by casting him into the raging sea. Reluctant to send him to his death, they attempted to row to safety—in vain. As a last resort, they did cast him overboard, with a prayer. "Do not make us guilty of innocent blood; for you, O Lord, have done as it pleased you" (1:14). The sea, immediately, grew calm and a grateful crew sacrificed to the Lord. They, not the Hebrew prophet, were rightfully acknowledging the God of Israel.

"The Lord provided a large fish to swallow up Jonah" (1:17). At this point, too often, the story breaks down. There has been so much vain speculation over that troublesome "whale." One feels that the author of Jonah chuckles over such silliness. In his story the "large fish" is God's submarine to get his reluctant prophet back on the job. We had left him, alone in the middle of the Mediterranean. He had to get back to the land of Israel: too far to swim. Hence the "large fish." It is not possible to ascertain whether the psalm (2:1-9) is an integral part of the writing or a later addition in view of the label: a prayer from "the belly of Sheol." The author has, assuredly, a refined sense of humor. The psalm may well come from him. Jonah had to have something to do during those three days and nights: He composed a psalm. At the end, the "submarine" landed him safely.

"The word of the Lord came to Jonah a second time" (3:1). This time he did set out for Nineveh. He had learned a lesson. He would find that his education had scarcely begun. It is a point of interest that while the "great fish" had aroused such curiosity, the immense size of the city—"an exceedingly large city, a three days' walk across" (3:3)—had raised little comment. Archaeology has shown Nineveh to be a modest town by our standards. Jonah walked a whole day through that narrative Nineveh before he felt he had got sufficiently into it to proclaim his message of woe: "Forty days more, and Nineveh shall be overthrown!" (3:4). Reaction was immediate and startling: universal assent and repentance. The Assyrian king, himself in sackcloth and ashes, proclaimed a total fast throughout the city. Even the animals should be clad in sackcloth—the author will have his joke. There is heavy irony. His readers would realize that their ancestors had not responded to the great prophets in quite the manner of those Ninevites—their response to Jeremiah, for instance. Now, when a Hebrew prophet spoke a word of the Lord, a pagan people jumped to attention. Their repentance and conversion were sincere and complete. "When God saw what they did, how they turned from their evil ways, God changed his mind about the calamity that he had said he would bring upon them; and he did not do it" (3:10). Here is the refreshing Hebrew God who can change his mind when he pleases.

As for Jonah: "This was very displeasing to Jonah, and he became angry" (4:1). It was as he had feared; it was why he had sought to evade the mission in the first place (4:2-3). But he had not given up hope. He went into the desert, east of the city, and sat, expectantly, in the shade of a hastily constructed shelter. If disaster did fall after all, he had a ringside seat. The Lord had a further lesson in store. With a twinkle in his eye, he caused a leafy tree to spring up over Jonah's vantage point. The prophet was thrilled with the shade and the coolness. Next day, the Lord caused the tree to shrivel and, to compound the misery, sent a *khamseen/sirocco,* the oppressive desert wind. An unhappy and thoroughly angry Jonah longed for the relief of death (4:6-8).

The Lord, solicitously, enquired of Jonah if he had good grounds for his anger. His fervent reply would sound, in colloquial terms, "Damn right, I have!" Then the lesson. Jonah had become all worked up over an ephemeral tree, with whose growth and fate he had had nothing to do. "And should not I be concerned about Nineveh, that great city, in which there are more than a hundred and twenty thousand persons who do not know their right hand from their left, and also many animals?" (4:11). Now we appreciate the earlier stress on the immensity of the city and the reference to animals (3:3,8). A city of such magnitude would, at any time, have upwards of 120,000 newborn babies. Could Jonah really expect that God would casually destroy all these innocents—and the unoffending animals? We are not told if Jonah had taken the lesson to heart. This story ending is an example (see Luke 15:11 -32) of the literary feature of unresolved conflict. Its purpose is to involve the reader/hearer. It challenges our response as we step into Jonah's shoes. We write its ending.

There can be little doubt that many to whom the story was first addressed would have found it disconcerting. They would have found the attitude of Nahum and Tobias more congenial. Yet, it is a story that might have been told by Jesus. He was "friend of sinners." His Father, he knew, was merciful and forgiving. He was a God too much for the "righteous." They could not stomach the scandalous message of the Son.

THE BARB

We have not finished with Jonah. The tragedy of his stance is caught in one astonishing statement. I have long been convinced of the critical importance of one's image of God. It is increasingly clear to me that the basic reason for the rejection, by the religious authorities and the God-fearing Pharisees, of the word and person of Jesus was the image of God that he proclaimed and manifested. The word of Jonah points firmly in the same direction. Jonah disclosed the reason for his initial flight. He had a nagging suspicion that, in sending him with stern warning to the Ninevites, his God had a hidden agenda. He feared that mercy and forgiveness might lurk within the word of threat. His worst fears had been realized.

> He prayed to the LORD and said, "O LORD! Is not this what I said while I was still in my own country? That is why I fled to Tarshish at the beginning: for I knew that you are a gracious God and merciful, slow to anger, and abounding in steadfast love, and ready to relent from punishing. And now, O LORD, please take my life from me, for it is better for me to die than to live." (4:2-3)

Jonah had fled his God. That was grave indeed—as the pagan sailors had understood. The enormity is that he had fled *this* God—a God gracious, merciful, of steadfast love!

There was the rub: infinite love, a love that knew no limit, no frontier. It was a love that embraced even the hated Ninevites. This was too much. In Johannine terms: "This is a hard saying, who can accept it?" (John 6:60). It is all too reminiscent of the reaction to the word and praxis of Jesus: "This fellow welcomes sinners and eats with them" (Luke 15:2). It has never been easy for the "righteous" to come to terms with an "unjust" God. Jonah, then, underlines the predictable human reaction to divine generosity. If God is generous to me—fine. He dare not be generous to those whom we have judged to be undeserving of his mercy. In short, our HOPE rests, solely, in our God. A God who is God of infinite love—*in-finitus*—without limit.

The New Testament

4. Image of the Invisible God

Faith

"*L*et us run with perseverance the race that is set before us, looking to Jesus the pioneer and perfecter of our faith" (Heb 12:1-2). For the author of Hebrews faith in Jesus the High Priest seated "at the right hand of the throne of God" (12:2) is what gives meaning to the Christian way. At the same time, no other New Testament writer has stressed more the humanity of this heavenly High Priest. For he has in sight a specific historical person: Jesus of Nazareth. Christianity, like every religion, has its myths, but it is not founded on myth. Yet, what came to be, after New Testament times, was ahistorical Christology that displayed little of the vulnerable Jesus who died on a cross. Even when the earthly Jesus was kept in view, there has been a tendency to detach the death of Jesus from his life and to detach the resurrection of Jesus from his career and death. To do so is to blunt the challenge of the prophet Jesus and, ultimately, to fail to grasp the saving significance of his death and the true meaning of his resurrection. We Christians cannot ever ignore Jesus. We have been brilliant in denying him.

In his person, Jesus of Nazareth embodies the riddle, the paradox of Christianity. Christianity is, or ought to be, a religion of wondrous hope. And so it is, for those who understand it. There has been much focus on the cross—rightly so. The Christian will always remember, however, that Easter Sunday stands beyond Good Friday. The Stations of the Cross do not end at the tomb. Our faith is Easter faith. Our hope is paschal hope.

To make our way to God, we must learn to accept that God has first made his way to us. The original sin was humankind's snatching at the wisdom that could only be gift (Gen 3:1-7). Humanity's sin continues to be an attempt to escape the ways of God. It has long perplexed and disturbed me that Old Testament men and women often had a deeper understanding of God, and certainly a more personal relationship with God, than has been the experience of many Christians. In Jesus of Nazareth the divine has entered into our world, our history. God has become one among us. But we would bypass the way of God. The primal temptation is still there: "...you will be like God." The basic Christian truth is: "I am the way" (John 14:6). If God's way to humankind is through the man Jesus, then our Christian way to God is through the human Jesus.

GOD WAS IN CHRIST

"God was in Christ, reconciling the world to himself" (2 Cor 5:19). This is arguably the very best Christological statement, and it weds Christology with soteriology. Where Jesus is, there is God; and God is God *for us*. But Jesus of Nazareth is the thoroughly human person who was "born of woman" (Gal 4:4), who lived in our world, who died, horribly, on a cross. We cannot *know* God. Yet, we meet God in Jesus. The author of Hebrews has told us in no uncertain terms: "When in times past God spoke to our forefathers, he spoke in many and various ways by the prophets." This is revelation of God indeed but fragmentary and mediated through *servants*. "[I]n these last days he has spoken to us by a *Son*....He is the reflection of God's glory, and the exact imprint of God's very being" (Heb 1:1-3 [italics added]). This Son, who is the whole word of God, is the Jesus who "had to become like his brothers and sisters in every respect....one who in every respect has been tested as we are, yet without sin" (2:17; 4:15).

If Jesus bears the stamp of God's very being, he does so as a human person, like us in all things. *Jesus* tells us what God is like. *Jesus* is God's summons to us, God's challenge to us. We can say, truly, that God is love; we have no idea what *divine* love is in itself. In Jesus we see God's love in action. We learn that God is a God who is with us in our suffering and our death. We are sure of it because of the suffering and death of Jesus.

In Jesus, God has shown himself in human form: "He is the image of the invisible God" (Col 1:15). In practice, we have slipped quickly past this human aspect. We have turned, instead, to a "divine icon" comfortably free of any trait of the critical prophet. We had consigned Jesus to his heavenly home. And wisely, because we had realized a long time ago that he is safer there! We genuflect before "our divine Lord" who does not impinge on us because of the manner in which we envisage him. He does not really have any critical impact on the life of our world. But Jesus of Nazareth is a very uncomfortable person to have about. There remains the Gospel and its challenge, its "dangerous memory."

To diminish the human reality of Jesus is to screen from sight the God who would shine through him. Christology has tended to do just that. It has done so because it has been so influenced by the image of a Greek God. Instead, we need to acknowledge a vulnerable Jesus if we are to meet our vulnerable God.[27] The mystery of Jesus is that in him God communicates himself in full and unrestricted manner. Jesus' divinity is not, as sometimes presented, a kind of second substance in him. His divinity consists in the fact that, as the perfect counterpart of God, he is the manifestation and presence of God in our world. Any misrepresentation that "Jesus is human, but...," and it is all too common, is, effectively, refusal of the God who revealed himself in Jesus. When the human Jesus is not acknowledged, our understanding of God suffers and our Christianity suffers. "The gospel is good news not just about Jesus but about the God of Jesus, the maker of heaven and earth, the God of all men and women....We Christians learn to express stammeringly the content of what 'God' is and the content of what 'humanity' can be from the career of Jesus."[28] Perhaps the most, and the best, that can be said is: Jesus is the human person in whom God is fully present.

Jesus Christ

The object of Christian faith is the person of Jesus Christ who once lived, briefly, on earth, in the first century A.D. and now lives on in the Father's presence. The subject matter of our Gospels is this Jesus Christ. The Gospels, at once historical and theological, proclaim Jesus of Nazareth as the Christ, the definitive revelation of God. The proclaimed Jesus is a construct of Christian theological and spiritual imagination aimed at eliciting a faith response. The proclamation embraces strictly historical elements (e.g., Jesus' death on the cross) and theological interpretation in terms of biblical categories (e.g., ascent to God's right hand).

The real or actual Jesus is the glorified Savior alive in our midst. He will always be shrouded in mystery. The total reality of any person is unknowable to human discernment—how much more the reality of the Risen One. The Gospels present us with "the earthly Jesus": a portrait of Jesus during his life on earth. Their partial, and theologically colored, pictures serve as the source for the theoretical construct, "the historical Jesus." The historical Jesus is not the real Jesus but only a fragmentary hypothetical reconstruction of him by modern means of research. But this reconstruction is of immense importance—particularly in our day. Jesus is an appealing and a challenging figure.

The historical Jesus is not coextensive with the Jesus of the Gospel narratives. There is much in the Gospel narratives that is not historical. The Gospel picture is "accurate" not in the sense that it is exact in detail but that it is truth-bearing. It is the acceptance of it by the early believing community that guarantees the substantial truth of the gospel account. The Gospel Jesus is more than the historical Jesus: The Gospel presents not only history but the transhistorical, not only fact but theological interpretation. On the other hand, the ecclesiastical proclamation of the Jesus-image is often less than, is unfaithful to, the historical Jesus in which the image is rooted.

The New Testament has a variety of Christologies. In practice, one of them has most markedly influenced later Christological speculation. It is needful to look, briefly, at Johannine Christology.

THE ONE SENT

The Fourth Gospel was a major factor in the elaboration of trinitarian theology and Christology at the Councils of Ephesus (431) and Chalcedon (451). For centuries it has been assumed that Chalcedon had spoken the definitive Christological word—all that remained was commentary. Christology became, in practice, a subtle word game around the formula of Chalcedon.[29] Whatever its influence on the councils, John's understanding of Jesus is quite independent of any later developments. On the other hand, the Fourth Gospel itself cannot be the starting point of Christology for the very good reason that it is not. The scholarly view is that John is the latest of our Gospels. Christology had begun even before Mark, our earliest Gospel. It had started with Paul, first and greatest Christian theologian. Still, the Fourth Gospel does merit our attention.

The distinctiveness of the Johannine Jesus is evident from the first line of the Fourth Gospel. He is the incarnate Logos—the human presence of God in the world. Jesus is the new temple: meeting place of God and humankind—the "place" of true worship (see John 2:13-22; 4:20-24). He has replaced the feasts of Israel; he is the Light of the world (chapters 7-9). He is the Good Shepherd who lays down his life for his sheep (chapter 10). He is the Way to the Father, the true Way, the Way of life (chapter 14). As genuine Vine he is Life-Source of his disciples (chapter 15). He is the One, lifted up from the earth, who draws all to himself (8:28; 12:32). He pours out the life-giving Spirit (7:37-39; 19:34-35).

As One come down from heaven, Jesus, from the start, seems an other-worldly figure. Admittedly, he can be found sitting wearily by a well (4:6). He is a man who "loved Martha and her sister and Lazarus" (11:5). But these are rare flashes. It is the majestic Word-made-flesh who moves through the pages of John. The passion narrative (chapters 18-19) effectively illustrates the distinctiveness of his Jesus. John presents the passion as the triumph of the Son of God. Jesus is firmly in control. He is the Judge who judges his judge (Pilate) and his accusers ("the Jews"). He is the King who reigns, with the cross for a throne.

All the while, for John, Jesus is the "one sent." He is agent of the Father, empowered to speak and act in the name of the Father. This role of agent explains otherwise contradictory statements in the Fourth Gospel. Tension is sharpest in the contrast of two terse declarations: "The Father and I are one" (10:30); "The Father is greater than I" (14:28). When we read them in the light of the role of agent and against other texts throughout the Gospel, we appreciate that there is no contradiction.

The Johannine Jesus is always conscious of being the "one sent." His statements are unambiguous: "I seek to do not my own will, but the will of him who sent me" (5:30). If he freely lays down his life, it is because, paradoxically, "I have received this command from my Father" (10:18). He is Son, apprenticed to his Father; he has learned everything from his Father: "The Son can do nothing on his own, but only what he sees the Father doing; for whatever the Father does, the Son does likewise" (5:19). "The Father loves the Son and shows him all that he himself is doing" (5:20). It is precisely because he is agent, plenipotent representative of the Father, that he is the living presence of that Father; he has received the Father's name and power. "Know and understand that the Father is in me and I in the Father" (12:38); "Whoever has seen me has seen the Father" (14:9). He is God's son because he is the one "whom the Father has sanctified and sent into the world" (10:36). Jesus speaks the I AM (8:24,28,58; 13:19) as the one who bears God's name and wields his power. In him God, the everlasting one, is revealed and made present. Revealer of the Father, Jesus is not identical with the Father. Here is where the statement, "The Father is greater than I" (14:28), fits in. The priority of the Father comes from the fact that Jesus' power comes from him. But what is one to make of the confession, "My Lord and my God" (20:28), at the close of the Gospel? Thomas was reacting, in wonder and praise, to the God who was so dramatically revealed in the risen Jesus.

THE LOGOS

There still remains the Word. A traditional starting point of Christology is the Johannine statement *ho logos sarx egeneto*—the Word became flesh, became a human person (John:1:14). The *logos,* the Word, was with God from the beginning and was God's agent in creation. The background here is Old Testament Wisdom; the figure of Wisdom is the most developed personification in Jewish tradition (alongside Word and Spirit). Wisdom is personification of God's own self—God's active and gracious presence in the world. (See Prov 8:22,27,30-31; Sirach 24:3,12; Wisdom 7:25-26.) In John the Logos assumes the role that had been attributed to Wisdom. Logos is God's commitment to be personally present in history. Jesus of Nazareth is the historical shape and form that God's eternal intent has taken. To gaze on the incarnate Word was to see the revelation of the divine in the human story.

As one who makes God uniquely present, as Revealer of God, Jesus is God's only Son. Perhaps the prologue of Hebrews puts the matter better. In the past God at various times and in several ways spoke through the prophets. In the fullness of time he has spoken in the person of his Son—who is "the reflection of God's glory and the exact imprint of God's very being" (Heb 1:3). Jesus is the manifestation and presence of God in our world.

The synoptists, like John, wrote out of their Easter faith but they, to an extent, have allowed the historical Jesus to be seen and to speak. John, for his part, has imposed wholly the Christ of faith upon the earthly Jesus. He has painted an icon. An icon does not aim at literal representation; it is consciously stylized. An icon brings out the spiritual significance of the subject. The Johannine icon, then, represents the Jesus of faith, the risen Lord. As well, the fourth evangelist has put into the mouth of Jesus the theological significance of what the earthly Jesus had meant. His Jesus is an icon of the Christ of faith; the words of his Jesus are words of the risen Lord. In short, the Johannine Jesus is the Christ of our postresurrection faith experience.[30]

THE CROSS

There needs to be a balance. It is found, notably, in Marcan Christology. For Mark, God was surely present in Jesus of Nazareth. His Jesus was the *man* who, at Gethsemane, besought his God to pass from him the cup of suffering, who experienced on that cross of suffering the awfulness of God-forsakenness. Mark's Christology was not Chalcedonian—it could not have been. His Christology is thoroughly Christian and profoundly challenging. Marcan Christology is not inferior to other New Testament Christologies. It is different. Christianity is about reality. Mark was a realistic theologian. In authentically Christian fashion his realism is manifest in his Christology—in his portrait of Jesus Christ.[31]

The scandal of Jesus' death remains. Paul had to wrestle with it. He had a name for the divine logic behind it: the *foolishness* of God. If, as a Jew, he had to struggle, painfully, with the obduracy of Israel, he had, again as a Jew, earlier come to terms with a deeper problem—that of a crucified Messiah. In Galatians he declared: "Christ redeemed us from the curse of the law by becoming a curse for us—for it is written, 'Cursed be everyone who hangs on a tree'" (3:13). There he admits to what, for any Jew, would appear to be a fatal rebuttal of the Christian claim that Jesus was Messiah. There was the contrary word of Torah, the unambiguous word of Deuteronomy: "When someone is convicted of a crime punishable by death and is executed, and you hang him on a tree, his corpse must not remain all night upon the tree; you shall bury him that same day, for anyone hung on a tree is under God's curse" (21:22-23).

In Christian tradition Jesus had been duly condemned to death by the high priest and the Sanhedrin as a "blasphemer" (Mark 14:63-64 and parallel texts). And he had been "hung on a tree"—crucified. Manifestly abandoned by God, he could not, by any logic, be God's Anointed One. It is evident that Paul who had been "a persecutor of the church" (Phil 3:6; see Gal 1:14,23) had, in face of the outrageous Christian claim, himself had to come to terms with the "scandal."

Paul, then, was acutely conscious of the formidable difficulty at the heart of the Christian message. If, at Caesarea Philippi, the reaction of Peter to the very suggestion that the Messiah might suffer and die was indignant denial (Mark 8:31-33), how much more unacceptable for any Jew to acknowledge as Messiah one whom God had abandoned to a shameful death. As for the non-Jew: It asked too much to recognize a savior in that helpless victim on a cross. When Paul declared: "We preach Christ crucified, a stumbling-block to Jews and folly to Gentiles" (1 Cor 1:23), he spoke from wry experience. He thought not only of the missionary challenge but, surely, recalled his personal conflict. He wanted to know nothing "except Jesus Christ and him crucified" (2:2) because it was just here he had come to discern the power and the wisdom of God (see 1:24). Nor does Paul view the resurrection of Jesus as a "saving operation." He would regard the resurrection as inherent in the cross.

The resurrection showed the cross in its true light and demonstrated that "God's foolishness is wiser than human wisdom, and

God's weakness is stronger than human strength" (1:25). Paul would not draw a veil over the scandal of the cross. Paul would not argue with the foolishness of God. In the scandal of the cross Jesus was authentic image of the all-mighty God—the God of infinite power who is never God of force. He was showing forth the true God of *infinite* love, compassion, forgiveness. We look to some ways in which Jesus achieved this even before the cross.

VINDICATOR OF THE POOR

Jesus had a free attitude to property. Himself of "lower middle-class" Galilean background—he was a *tekton*, an artisan (Mark 6:3)—he took for granted the owning of property. When he began his ministry and had abandoned his trade, he was supported in his itinerant mission by well-to-do women disciples (Luke 8:2-3). He urged that elderly parents must be supported from their children's means (Mark 7:9-13) and recommended that possessions be used to help the needy (12:41-42). In requiring money to be lent even without hope of return (Matt 5:42), Jesus was presupposing surplus funds that could be lent. The chief tax collector Zacchaeus was ready to give half his possessions to the poor (Luke 10:8-9). Jesus was invited to dinner by the rich and privileged (Luke 7:36; 14:1,12). In the parable of the laborers in the vineyard he has the employer declare: "Am I not allowed to do what I choose with what belongs to me?" (Matt 20:15). While all of this may not, as such, go back in detail to Jesus himself, there is a pattern that surely reflects his attitude.

On the other hand, Jesus himself, during his itinerant mission, had no possessions. And he did, with severity, attack wealth where it had captured people's hearts and had blinded their eyes to God's purpose. He had especially in mind surplus wealth: The rich ought to use their wealth to benefit the poor. An aspect of the camel saying—"It is easier for a camel to go through the eye of a needle than for someone who is rich to enter the kingdom" (Mark 10:25 and parallel texts)—is that it expresses the real difficulty the rich have in freeing themselves of possessiveness.

The Poor

Jesus knew it to be his vocation to proclaim the true God—the Father. He knew that in faithfulness to his task he was making the kingdom present. How he saw his task is vividly portrayed in Luke's introduction of Jesus' ministry (Luke 4:16–21). In his programmatic statement Jesus pointed to the recipients of his good news: captives, blind, oppressed—all who are weakest and powerless. They are "the poor." The "poor" are not only those with few or no possessions, and not only those whose poverty is "spiritual." In the biblical context the poor are the "little people" who are incapable of standing up for themselves and hence, by reason of their need and sorry state, are God's protected ones. The designation "poor" (as in Luke's beatitudes for instance, Luke 6:20–26) is not idealization: The poor really do need help; the hungry stand in need of nourishment; the mourning are visibly sorrowing. All cry out for compassion. The "poor" to whom Jesus announced the good news of the kingdom and whom he pronounced "blessed" are not those whom he proposed as models of virtue but are persons literally "down and out." The kingdom of God, the consolation of the new age, is granted to the weak and despised—to those who suffer, who weep, who sorrow.

The Beatitudes

Our gospels have two notably different versions of the beatitudes: Matthew 5:3-12 and Luke 6:20-23. Matthew has nine beatitudes. Luke has four—but with corresponding "woes" (Luke 6:24-26). Both versions have grown from an original core going back to Jesus, the additions and adaptations being due to the evangelists (or the traditions they had inherited). We can, without much trouble, discern a form of the beatitudes that would stand as a common basis for the development of the evangelists and that may reasonably be regarded as the beatitudes of Jesus. These are three:

> Blessed are the poor, for the kingdom is theirs.
> Blessed are those who hunger, for they will be filled.
> Blessed are the afflicted, for they will be comforted.

The beatitudes do not refer to three different categories but to three aspects of the same distressful situation. The first sets the tone. In declaring the poor blessed, Jesus gives concrete expression to the good news that he brings to the poor. The other two beatitudes make precise, and develop, the context of the first. In the Gospels, the poor are the indigent, those who depend totally on alms—they are the hungry, those who grieve over their unhappy lot. The most important text of the earliest Jesus tradition is this beatitude addressed to the poor. It is a fulfillment of Isaiah 61:1—"He has sent me to bring good news to the oppressed"—a promise that the wretched lot of the poor will be reversed under the reign of God. In Palestine, poor Jews were coming together as followers of Jesus—responding to his theology of liberation. Their present experience of poverty, hunger and tears played a decisive part in determining the object of their hope: They fervently longed that their lot would be reversed (see Luke 1:52–53). Jesus was hope of the poor.

Greed

A request by "someone in the crowd" for a ruling in a matter of inheritance (Luke 12:13), occasioning a warning against greed or cupidity (v. 15), constitutes the setting of the parable of the rich fool (12:16–21). The parable illustrates the peril to which *pleonexia*, "greed" or "covetousness," exposes one. In verse 21, the conclusion of the parable, Luke spoke his verdict: "So it is with those who store up treasures for themselves but are not rich toward God." The man had failed to take the positive ethical steps that a rich Christian must take to be saved. Jesus went on (12:22–24) to outline his demands on disciples and to sketch their corresponding lifestyle, wholly at odds with that of the rich man.

The error of the rich man lay, positively, in having thought only of his "soul"—his self-centeredness. He had stored up his harvest in view of having a good time for the rest of his life (12:19). His attitude might well be that of the discontented heir (v. 13; see 15:12–13). It corresponded to the outlook of people who are preoccupied with where to dine and what to wear (v. 22). It was the attitude of pagans

(v. 30). The error of the unhappy man comprised three factors: forgetfulness of God, forgetfulness of eternal life and forgetfulness of his obligation to the poor. He was truly a "fool" because he had not known how to use wisely the wealth he enjoyed.

The parable of the rich fool, which warns against the tendency to seek security in wealth, should not be taken in isolation from the following development (12:22–24). Here, addressing his *disciples,* Jesus put them on their guard, not against the danger of wealth (no immediate threat to them), but simply against the normal anxiety of the poor, that for basic needs. In dreaming of his full barns, the rich man had a sense of *security* (v. 19). The disciples, who possess nothing, vividly feel their insecurity (vv. 22,29). There is no question of condemning a longing for security inherent in the human condition. Rather, the intention is to show that the need goes astray when it seeks its sole support in earthly resources. There is no authentic security that is not founded on God, on a vivid consciousness of his parentlike solicitude.

In the parable there is no suggestion that wealth is evil in itself, independently of the disposition it may engender. Wealth is misfortune when it not only makes one indifferent to the good of the future life and when it distracts the rich from concern for the poor. It also tends to foster a sense of security incompatible with that trust which God claims for himself alone. In contrast, a "little flock" in a hostile world, disciples should not be discouraged but should look in trust to a Father who has chosen them for his kingdom (v. 32). The closing admonition puts the matter in a nutshell: "Where your treasure is, there your heart will be also" (v. 34). If the heart is set on the kingdom (v. 31) then one will have the right perspective.

Social Ethics

Luke, author of Luke-Acts, had in view a group living as an independent community—or a close-knit group of communities—in a city of the Roman Empire. While it did not have members from the upper classes, it did not have destitute people either—beggars and so on. There were, nonetheless, serious tensions within the community. These were due, on the one hand, to economic differences: In addition to rich people there were others who, while not destitute, were poor—ordinary folk such as manual workers and the like. On the other hand, there were social tensions. Wealthy and respectable Christians looked down on the less well-off. It was a feature of their Hellenistic culture.

At the center of the social message of Jesus in Luke are the instructions to the rich and respectable. They were offered a striking example in the person of Zacchaeus, the despised chief tax collector. He renounced half his possessions: "...half of my possessions I will give to the poor" (19:8). The Lucan Jesus might have added, as after the parable of the Good Samaritan, "Go and do likewise" (10:37). The duty of the rich is not to amass wealth for themselves but to be rich in God's sight—that is, to espouse the cause of the poor. Luke, as "evangelist of the rich," does not mince words. He desires the salvation of the rich but he is convinced that it can be achieved only through radical renunciation of the wealth that he perceives to be a formidable obstacle: "It is easier for a camel to go through the eye of a needle than for someone who is rich to enter the kingdom of God" (18:25).

When one takes Acts into account, one becomes acutely aware that Luke has a social goal in view: an equal distribution of property within the Christian community. In his picture of the first Christian community in Jerusalem he formulated his utopian vision of a group characterized by economic and social equality.

> All who believed were together and had all things in common; they would sell their possessions and goods and distribute the proceeds to all, as any had need. (Acts 2:44–45)

> Now the whole group of those who believed were of one heart and soul, and no one claimed private ownership of any possessions, but everything they owned was held in common....There was not a needy person among them, for as many as owned lands and houses sold them and brought the proceeds of what was sold. They laid it at the apostles' feet, and it was distributed to each as any had need. (4:32–37)

Likely, Luke knew little about the actual situation in the earliest community. Indeed he more than suggests that conditions may have been a good deal less rosy (e.g., 6:1). He painted an idealized picture: not as the first community was, but as he wanted his community to be. The real background to his idealized presentation was the deficiencies in his own community—at least what he regarded as deficiencies. The disturbing factor is that Luke's utopia catches, accurately, the vision of Jesus. For Jesus had about him a community of equals. He had explicitly rejected the social pattern of the world: "It shall not be so among you..." (Mark 10:43; Luke 22:26).

Evangelist of the Rich

Luke is evangelist of the rich and respected. This is to say, he wants to motivate them toward conversion in keeping with the social message of Jesus. If he is "evangelist of the rich," his message is challenge—not at all palatable to the wealthy. He is an exceptionally keen critic of the rich. But he does envisage their conversion, which, as he sees it, is possible only by way of radical renunciation—renunciation of half their possessions (or, ideally, of all of them), and by painful specific conduct—risky loans and cancellation of debts, for example. The Lucan attitude toward material possessions is not uncomplicated. One may discern a twofold stance: a moderate approach that advocates a measured generosity in favor of the less fortunate and a radical approach that recommends the renunciation of all wealth and possessions. One feels that Luke's own perspective is uncomplicated: The only sensible thing to do with money is to give it away in alms. But he is candid enough to acknowledge that his is not the only view and he leaves place, in his Gospel, for a moderate approach (see 19:8).

Women

We have looked at the "poor" mainly in terms of the economically poor. The term can carry a wider brief and include the marginalized. In the world of the day, women fell into that category. The Gospel of Luke contains more material about women than the other Gospels together. It insists that those who followed Jesus were both men and women: 8:1–3; 23:49; 24:9–11. While women are not correspondingly present in Acts, the believing community is regularly described as "men and women" (Acts 5:14; 8:3,12; 9:2,36–42). A group of men and women together had made up Jesus' followers. Later, men and women constituted the community of those who believed in Jesus.

In Luke 8:2–3 the women (Mary, Joanna, Susanna and "many others"), healed by Jesus, served him and his disciples out of their resources. *Diakonein* means "to serve" with the connotation of waiting on someone. It was a traditional term of service for slaves and women. Jesus transformed the meaning of the term. "Who is greater, the one who is at table or the one who serves? Is it not the one at the table? But I am among you one who serves" (Luke 22:27). The Christian leader is to be "like one who serves" (v. 26). *Ho diakonōn* (one who serves) is now an honorific designation. The antithetical roles of servant and ruler are paradoxically coupled. To serve (*diakonein*), a function proper to women, is applied to men who have a leadership role. It characterizes the manner in which leadership ought to be exercised. It is obvious that, along the lines of this model, women should readily qualify for leadership. This did not happen. Instead we find that, in Acts, the serving terminology is applied exclusively to men. It means that, in practice, women who supported and served (*diakonein*) were excluded from leadership. Leadership positions were de facto reserved for men.

There is an intriguing factor. Luke gives in Acts 1:22–23 his criteria for being an apostle: "So one of the men who had accompanied us during all the time that the Lord Jesus went in and out among us, beginning from the baptism of John until the day when he was taken up from us—one of these must become a witness with us to the resurrection." Admittedly, the issue is the replacement of Judas in order to complete the number of the Twelve. Yet, the requirement does fit Luke's own understanding of "apostle" in a wider sense. One must have been a disciple of Jesus from Galilee to Jerusalem. The women disciples ought to be obvious candidates (see Luke 8:2–3; 23:55–56; 24:1–11,22; Acts 1:14). They were excluded by an initial demand of maleness: "one of the *men*." There is no logic here. There is prejudice. Women appeared as the first witnesses of the Lord's resurrection—Luke 24:1-12. They spoke the truth, they fulfilled the demand of Deuteronomy 19:15 as to the acceptable number of witnesses: two, or better, three— there were several women (Luke 24:10). Yet, they were not believed. The reaction of the "apostles" was spontaneous: "These words seemed to them an idle tale, and they did not believe them" (v. 11). A whole group of women (v. 10) stood over against the whole group of men ("the eleven and all the rest," v. 9). The detailed testimony ("all these things," v. 9) was refused, the women were rejected. The women had been confirmed as disciples: The message of the resurrection was addressed directly and completely to them. This was confirmation of their privileged place among the followers of Jesus. They were not acknowledged simply and solely because they were women.

> When women in Acts are excluded from becoming apostles or from being leaders in other ways, this is a consequence of Luke's restricted and special concept of apostleship and acceptance of the public sphere as a man's world. So the public act of witness has to be carried out by men. This is nowhere justified in theological terms, and women are never explicitly adjured to keep silence or to be subordinate. What is demonstrated is a structure imposing silence. The narrative about the women on Easter morning shows this with considerable clarity (Luke 24:4-11). When the message fails to reach its destination, this is not due to the women, but because the men do not believe them. But this does not shake the relationship of power and the conclusion is therefore none the less a rejection of women's possibility to bear witness.[32]

Luke, in his two-volume work, conveys a double message. In his Gospel he preserves strongly positive traditions about women and intimates an active role for them. He then reveals that male bias militated against a like role. The Gospel evidence is that Jesus' own attitude to women was unconventionally positive. Paul had welcomed women as fellow ministers. The change came about when the patriarchal household system was adopted as the model for the Christian community structure (see 1 Tim 2:8-3:13; Titus

2:1-10). Women were effectively marginalized.[33] Despite, however, the situation evident throughout Acts, Luke has given a glimpse of an alternative route. His "double message nurtures a dangerous remembrance."[34] This excursus on women is not irrelevant. If spirituality is faith lived out in love, it must face up to any manifestation of injustice.

Christian "Pharisees"

Luke had to face the problem of wealth in his own community. If there were no absolutely needy members, there were those relatively well-off. These were, by and large, the "Pharisees"; significantly, Luke characterized the historical Pharisees as "lovers of money" (16.14). He was perceptively aware of two attitudes fostered by riches: a false sense of security and a lack of appreciation of and concern for the plight of the poor (see 12:16-21; 16:19-31). Indeed, he was conscious that mammon might become one's god—"You cannot *serve* God and mammon" (16:13). He also had to inculcate the practice of almsgiving among people for whom almsgiving was not part of their culture—almsgiving was not known among Greco-Romans. For that matter, Luke was convinced that relief of human need and suffering was the one, the only, positive contribution of money—"...you must give up all that you have" (18:22).

We do not know if his "Pharisees" responded. His remains a valid Christian option—it inspired Francis of Assisi. The New Testament gives ample evidence of broad pluralism; there are many ways of being Christian. But there are limits. Wealth should be a source of discomfort for one striving to live a Christian way. Indeed, any factor or attitude—power, wealth, prestige or whatever—that fails to value people first and before all else is incompatible with the call of Jesus. "Seek first the rule of God...." And the rule of God, the kingdom, is God as salvation for humankind. This is *the* message of Jesus.

Salvation for *humankind*. There is, insistently, the place of women in the Church. It is a problem that cannot be wished away. Jesus came to bring good news to the poor, to welcome captives, to

77

free the oppressed (Luke 4:18). It cannot be his will that his sisters remain second-class citizens in an institution that purports to be his *ekklēsia*. The patriarchal model does not square with his teaching and practice. Only an assembly of brothers *and* sisters can truly constitute his Church.

FRIEND OF SINNERS

In chapters 1 through 3 of Romans the apostle Paul painted, in stark color, the fate of humankind enslaved to *hamartia*—sin. He did so as foil to divine generosity: "God proves his love for us in that while we were sinners Christ died for us" (Rom 5:8). The offer of God's forgiveness was distinctive of Jesus' ministry. Indeed, he won notoriety as "friend of sinners." Traditionally, the challenge of Jesus has been modified in every conceivable manner. Here is a case in point. Jesus welcomed sinners—without condition. This was shockingly unconventional and a scandal to the righteous. Jesus was too much for the religious authorities of his day. He seems to be too much for the religious authorities of any day. Always, it seems, sinners can find that gap and encounter the gracious forgiveness and welcome of the Father/Mother—ever to the discomfiture of the righteous.

> Why does he eat with tax collectors and sinners?...Those who are well have no need of a physician, but those who are sick; I came not to call the righteous, but sinners. (Mark 2:16–17)

Jesus was friend of sinners. The text witnesses to a conflict between the Jesus movement and other Jews on the issue. Similarly we may take it that those addressed in Matthew 21:31 ("Truly, I say to you, the tax collectors and the harlots go into the kingdom of God before you") are Jews who deny to tax collectors and sinners the right to hope in God's forgiveness. The offense of the statement is its clear implication that the wretched prostitutes and detested tax collectors, scorned by the refined and religious, are preferred by God to their despisers. Pharisees would be prepared to accept that God is merciful to sinners; they would not accept the unconditional forgiveness of God implicit in the role of

Jesus. In the earliest Jesus movement the Pharisees are not yet representatives of a Judaism hostile to Christianity. They are Jews who perceived that the Jesus movement was making an enormous and, to them, unacceptable claim. It was claiming that God takes the part of the poor and the outcast—simply because they are poor, deprived and despised. The rule of God was being inaugurated among the lowly and despised—not among the "righteous." That they could not and would not accept. At a further level Jesus is rejecting any labeling or categorizing of people as "sinners."

Mercy

Their Lucan setting (15:1-2) would fix the three parables of mercy (15:4-7, 8-10, 11-32) credibly in the ministry of Jesus. The "grumbling" of verse 2—"The Pharisees and the scribes were grumbling and saying, 'This fellow welcomes sinners and eats with them'"—speaks so much. The Pharisees had set the Torah as the way of righteousness and had found in meticulous observance of it the achievement of righteousness. All who did not know the Law, or who did not keep it, were "sinners," strangers to the way of righteousness. "But this crowd, which does not know the Law— they are accursed" (John 7:49). Jesus staunchly refused to categorize people; to him no one was outcast. The Pharisees could not bear that Jesus welcomed "sinners" and sought them out. Worst of all, and there is a note of disgust, if not a tone of horror: He "eats with them" (see 5:30; 7:34). It was axiomatic that one could not have communion with "sinners": Contact with these outcasts rendered one ritually unclean. What right had Jesus to flout so basic a requirement of the broader Torah?[35]

Jesus countered their accusations by telling a parable (15:3)— three parables in fact: the lost sheep, the lost coin and the lost son. His defense was that he sought and welcomed the outcast because such is the Father's will. God is vindicator of the poor; the faithful Son was vindicator in turn. The outcasts, too, had caught the message. All their lives they had been told that they stood beyond the pale. They were without hope, robbed of hope by the "righteous." Only an infinitely gracious God can forgive the devastation visited, throughout history, by the "righteous" on "sinners," in particular by "righteous" with pastoral responsibility.

The plight of the "outcasts" is well documented in the Pharisee and the tax collector (18:10-14). "The tax collector, standing far off, could not even look up to heaven, but was beating his breast and saying, 'God, be merciful to me, a sinner!'" At the end of all, he could not really bring himself to accept that God was as the righteous had painted him. At least he dared to hope that it was not so. Now, such as he were given glowing hope. This man of God, unlike the righteous, did not shun them. No wonder that "sinners" looked to Jesus. And he, insultingly branded a "friend of sinners," would have accepted the designation as the truest compliment. His meat was to do the will of him who sent him (John 4:34). Nothing was dearer to the Father's heart than this loving concern for the outcast.

Jesus had table fellowship with "tax collectors and sinners." He, in a manner that they could understand, assured them that God loved them. Doubtless, he hoped that they would change their ways, but he did not threaten. And he did not demand that they perform what the Law stipulated if they were to be reckoned as righteous. In spite of Luke's own emphasis on repentance, the distinctive, and scandalous, conduct of Jesus himself shines through his narrative. When one looks beyond Luke, it is evident that Jesus cannot be characterized as a preacher of repentance. He was, emphatically, preacher of forgiveness. One thinks, for instance, of Zacchaeus in his sycamore tree. A preacher of repentance might have wagged the finger and read him the riot act—a spectacularly captive hearer. Instead, Jesus casually invited himself to dinner in his home. Zacchaeus must nearly have toppled from his perch in surprised delight. A sermon would have left him unaffected—he had been too often preached at. The novel approach changed his life (19:1-10).

The Lost Son

While the parable of the lost son (15:11-32), in its present shape, is surely a composition of Luke, his inspiration was, authentically, Jesus. Only the conviction that he echoed the sentiment of a wholly merciful Savior could account for the subversive, and wondrously comforting, tenor of this powerful story. The story of the father and his two sons is allegory; the characters are God, the sinner and the righteous. Jesus' purpose was not only to depict God's gracious forgiveness. It was to hold the mirror up to his opponents. It was to challenge them to see themselves in the elder son. Jesus' parable is a defense of his conduct, his concern for the "little ones" whom the Pharisees had written off as outcasts. Defense, yes—yet profoundly challenging.

"There was a man who had two sons." The younger of the brothers asked his father for the share of the family property that would fall to him—a third of the estate. He evidently turned his share into cash and set off. His money was quickly squandered in dissolute living, and his erstwhile friends left him in the lurch. He had struck rock bottom: a Jew herding pigs. He even envied the pigs, who had something to eat. He cannot share *their* meal; he cannot have table fellowship with pigs! In his degradation he "came to himself." And his thought was of his father. He will return, confess his folly, acknowledge his unworthiness. Maybe he will be received back as a "hired hand."

"He got up and went." That is what the father had longed for. Ever on the lookout, he spied the hapless homecomer and hastened to welcome him. Not a word of reproof. Stirred only by loving compassion, he embraced and kissed the lost one. *All* was forgiven. The son's little speech was no longer confession (as his rehearsed speech was intended to be); it was spontaneous response to forgiveness. There were no strings to this forgiveness. Best robe, signet ring, shoes: The youth was reinstated. He was son as though he had never left, had never gone astray. Nor is this the end. It was a moment to be savored, a time for joymaking. Such is God's forgiveness, Jesus says. God casts our sins behind his back; he buries them in the deeps of the sea (see Isa 38:17; Mic 7:18–19).

Jesus' Jewish readers would have grasped the pathos of the young man's plight. What they would have found disconcerting was the incredible conduct of the father. To receive back, without a word of reproof and without any condition at all, one who had

81

shown himself so weak and untrustworthy was incredibly foolish. They would have identified, readily, with the hardnosed other son. Yet, the fact that the story itself manifestly extolled the conduct of the father would have given pause. What is it all about? It is too much for humankind, as the second part of the parable brings out.

The Begrudger

In readings of the lost son the elder son of the story regularly gets short shrift. This is unfortunate because he is, indeed, the focus of the story. The first part of this little drama portrays God's gracious forgiveness. "I will go to my father"—nothing more is needed. The father had taken over. The sinner was warmly welcomed and reinstated without condition; it was a moment to be celebrated. The other son, the righteous, was scandalized and hurt: it is not fair! There is just his error: He had not understood that God is *not* fair! God is wholly merciful, boundless in his forgiveness. "Justice" does not enter into it. The Father who had embraced the sinner is gentle, too, with the aggrieved righteous one. "Son, you are always with me, and all that is mine is yours."

He is no worse off because God is merciful. What is in question is recognition of a merciful God. And this recognition has to be painfully practical. The elder son had washed his hands of his brother. The unwelcome and unwelcomed homecomer was "this son of yours." He is, by his father, delicately but unmistakably put right: The homecomer is "this brother of yours." And he was invited to enter into the celebration: "We had to celebrate and rejoice." The ending of the story offers a classic example of the literary feature of unresolved conflict. Its purpose is to involve the reader or hearer. We are made to wonder how we might act in the place of the elder brother. Will I stay outside, sulking? Will I welcome my sister or brother and share the joy of our Parent? In effect, *I* must write the ending of this story. My ending will depend on my understanding of God—my image of God.

On many counts this is a disturbing story for us Christians of today. Luke took it out of the ministry of Jesus and addressed it directly to "Pharisees" in his own Christian community. And, surely, we must look to ourselves, to our possible resentment at God's graciousness to sinners. We can find comfort in the warm treatment of the younger son. Always, there is the Father. He is the real challenge. Our gracious and forgiving God holds the stage. This story persuasively shows God's loving concern for humankind and, in particular, his favoritism toward the outcast. It sets a question mark against the theology of forgiveness reflected in much of our penitential practice. God's forgiveness seems too good to be true. Above all, there is the uncomfortable message that one really comes to understand this Father only by acknowledging the brother and sister as brother and sister—a lesson learned by the author of 1 John: "Those who do not love a brother or sister whom they have seen cannot love God whom they have not seen" (4:20).

5. The Challenge

COMING TO FAITH

esus began his mission by summoning disciples. The call of the first disciples (Mark 1:16-20) is a passage shaped to bring out the nature of Jesus' call and of the Christian response— to show what "following Jesus" means. The decisive factor is the person of Jesus himself. In order to become a disciple of Jesus it is not necessary to be an exceptional person. It was the impression of Jesus on Peter and his companions, reinforced by his personal word of call, that brought them into his following and made them his disciples. Mark was not intent on describing a scene from the ministry of Jesus. Rather, he was more concerned with the theological dimension of a typical call to discipleship.

In this context of discipleship the passage Mark 15:40-44 is of utmost significance. Mark says of the little group of women who witnessed the execution of Jesus: "They used to follow him and provided for him when he was in Galilee; and there were many other women who had come up with him to Jerusalem" (v. 41). The women had "followed him"—*akolouthein* is a technical term for discipleship. Although this is the only place in the Gospel where the discipleship of women is mentioned in explicit terms, we should not overlook the reference to "many women." We must recognize that throughout the Gospel "disciple" is an inclusive term. It is because they had continued to follow him if only "at a distance" (v. 40)—as women they could not be at the very place of execution—that the final message is entrusted to these women (16:1-8). They alone, of all disciples, had followed to the cross. Luke is the evangelist who gets the credit for alerting us to Jesus' solicitude for womankind. But Mark had, beforehand, made his telling contribution. These women disciples had stood steadfast and have not been ashamed of Jesus. They are those of whom the Son of Man will not be ashamed (8:38).

Messiah

Mark's Christians were followers of Jesus, who believed that he is Christ and Son of God. Yet, they had much to learn. The evangelist set out to declare who Jesus is, to spell out the nature of his messiahship. It is easy enough, he realizes, to declare, even with conviction: You are the Messiah. What matters is how one understands that confession. It does not ask too much of one to be the willing disciple of a risen Lord. We, all of us, find triumph and glory congenial. Mark takes an uncompromising stand. Jesus is, of course, Messiah and Son of God; he is the one who will, without fail, come to gather his elect (Mark 13:26-27). But he is, too, the suffering Son of Man, who walked a lonely path to his death, who died, as it seemed to him, abandoned even by God. Mark stresses that only one who has come to terms with the cross can understand the resurrection of the Lord. Jesus was one who was glorified because he had accepted the *kenōsis*, the self-abasement, of his life and death. That is why Jesus was, for the first time, formally acknowledged by a human as Son of God as he hung lifeless on the tree (15:39).

Jesus was Messiah, of that Mark was sure—but he is a disconcerting Messiah. The question stands, writ large: Who, then, is this? That Jesus would have permitted himself to be taken by his enemies, to be maltreated and mocked by them, and put to death, is something that the contemporaries of Jesus and the readers of Mark could hardly comprehend. Yet, if one has not come to terms with this "scandal," one has not grasped the originality of Jesus, in particular, the Jesus portrayed by Mark. Jesus did not come as judge with sentence and punishment for those who would not receive the gift of forgiveness and salvation he offered them. He had come as the one who would let himself be crushed by the evil intent of those who resisted him and would be rid of him.

Prophet and Teacher

In Jesus the roles of prophet and teacher overlapped—as they did, regularly, in the prophets of Israel. Jesus taught distinctively. And he taught with authority. As a first-century Palestinian Jew he, of course, shared much of the theology of his tradition. But there was more than enough to set him apart. The ultimate factor was his understanding of God. Clashes with his religious opponents over matters of law, such as sabbath observance, were symptomatic of fundamental difference. Jesus knew, better than any other, that to proclaim one's belief in God is not enough. What matters, and matters utterly, is the kind of God in whom one believes. It makes, literally, a world of difference whether one's God is the true God or a distorted image of that God. For Jesus, God is God of humankind. God is found where there is goodness and a striving for the liberation of humankind. We are human beings, created in the image of God; we are meant to image God. Our destiny is to be human—as God understands humanness. The corollary is that only with God can we reach full humanness. Jesus, with God, reached whole humanness.

As teacher, no less than as prophet, Jesus sought disciples. He called, and his call was a powerful summons. Discipleship meant wholehearted commitment—it was no soft option. His principle was that religion was meant to enable men and women to attain authentic humanness; it was not meant to enslave them. He took a firm stand against legalism. In light of God's preferential option for the poor, he warned of the threat of riches. Jesus showed no favoritism. His declaration, "It is easier for a camel to go through the eye of a needle than for someone who is rich to enter the kingdom of God" (10:245), would not be welcome in certain quarters. The gist of his teaching is found in his startling assertion that the essence of authority is service. If this were grasped and lived, much else would fall together. Until it is truly grasped and lived, authority in the Church will continue to forfeit respect. Service (*diakonia*) should be the characteristic mark of a Christian community. A peculiarly appropriate service is the offer and practice of forgiveness.

Forgiveness

Just as ben Sirach regarded forgiveness of our neighbor as criti-
cally important for right human conduct (Sir 28:2-4), so
Matthew underlined its significance for the early Church. The
passage in Matthew 18:21-35 forms the conclusion of Matthew's
community discourse (chapter 18). Though he had to face the
uncomfortable prospect that an unrepentant brother or sister
might have to be excluded from the community (18:15-20), he
wants to ensure that his word on relationships within the community will end on the resounding note of forgiveness.

"Then Peter came and said to him. 'Lord, if another member of
the church sin against me, how often should I forgive? As many as
seven times?' Jesus said to him, 'Not seven times, but, I tell you,
seventy times seven.'" While Luke (Luke 17:4) also contains the
first saying about forgiveness, Matthew adds special importance
to it in three ways: by putting the question in the mouth of Peter,
leader of the Christian community; by increasing the number of
times from seven to seventy times seven—an unlimited number of
times; by adding a parable, as he likes to do at the end of a discourse, to drive the point home.

The disparity between the two sums mentioned in the parable
(Matt 18:23-34) is gigantic—ten thousand talents is an unimagin-
able sum; a denarius is a laborer's daily wage. A debt impossible
of repayment is written off, casually, by the king, and the man is
not even sacked. It is quite the situation one finds in Luke
15:11-24. Yet, one who had been shown such mercy cannot find it
in his heart to remit a paltry debt. Not only that: He will not even
give his fellow-servant—his social equal—reasonable time and
opportunity to repay. The king who had been moved with "pity"
(Matt 18:27) is now "angry" (v. 34).

The parable is a thinly veiled allegory. The "servant" is the sinner; his situation is hopeless. The "king" is a merciful God who
freely and lovingly forgives any sin. Luke has painted the warmer
picture of prodigal Father and wayward child (Luke 15:11-24). The
reality is the same in either case. Like the younger son in the Lucan
parable, this man, too, is forgiven with no strings attached. Faced
with a cry of desperation, the forgiving God was moved with pity

(Matt 18:27). But when the recipient of such forgiveness cannot find it in his heart to be merciful, the master is angry (18:33). Response to God's gracious forgiveness cannot be payment of a debt that is already fully remitted. It is, instead, warm thanksgiving for the blessing of such forgiving love. And the story in Matthew underlines again that sin, as God regards it, is man's inhumanity to man (even more sadly, man's inhumanity to woman) whatever shape that may take. Our abuse of others (and of ourselves) is an affront to the loving Parent who counts us as his children. Jesus clearly understood this because he knew his Father. A corollary. Jesus asks us, frail humans, to be forgiving without limit. He dares to ask the impossible because he knew that his God is an *Abba* whose forgiveness literally knows no limit.

Prayer

Prayer is a Christian need. We are children of God and should turn, with childlike directness, to our Parent. In this world we are sisters and brothers of the Brother who walked his way to Calvary. The Christian way, lived beforehand by Jesus, so firmly proposed by him and by his earliest disciples, is a way that challenges us. It is a way we dare not walk alone. But we are not alone, for he is with us. We meet him in our prayer and keep step with him on the way. He has taught us to pray to the Father, and we have learned to pray to him.

"Descended from David according to the flesh" (Rom 1:3), Jesus was a son of Israel. As a committed Israelite he was, by definition, a man of prayer. Aside from Luke, who had a special interest in prayer, the evangelists do not elaborate on Jesus' prayer life. That is not surprising. Simply, they, like him, took prayer for granted. We, Christians of another culture and of the twenty-first century, cannot be so casual. We demand reasons for everything and we do ask why we ought to pray in the first place. The realization that Jesus was a man of prayer may give us food for thought.

Mark, with attractive candor, tells us that Jesus' addiction to prayer was something of a trial to his disciples. The evangelist has given a sample day in the early Galilean ministry, at Capernaum

(Mark 1:21-34), a day of enthusiastic reception and of great promise. His disciples, caught up in the excitement, were chagrined when Jesus went missing (v. 37)–"In the morning, while it was still very dark, he got up and went out to a deserted place, and there he prayed" (1:35). Typically, Mark has said much in few words. Jesus had slept (he "got up"), had snatched a few hours of sleep. For his mission he needed deeper refreshment, a more potent source of energy, and he found it in prayer to his *Abba*. As one "like us in every respect" (Heb 2:17), Jesus was wholly dependent on this God. He turned, spontaneously, to an *Abba* who would support him, who would back him in his endeavors. True, he was sent, one who had to plow his own furrow. But he was not alone because the Father was with him. The prayer of Jesus, his whole prayerful trust in his *Abba,* is an essential ingredient of any meaningful Christology. And it is an incentive to us in our prayer endeavor.

Prayer of and by Jesus, by example rather than contrived design, is meant to alert the disciple to his or her dependence on God. If the Son found a need and a joy in converse with his Father, he could expect that the other children of God, his sisters and brothers, would, too, experience that need and that happiness. The comforting fact is that Jesus, as our high priest, has not ended his prayer. Now with the Father, he has no need, any more, to pray for himself. Henceforth, he is the high priest who prays *for* us, who makes intercession for us, without respite (see Heb 7:25).

Conviction of the companionship of God was the secret of Jesus' own prayer life. What was it that moved him to mark his prayer with the new, intimate mode of address: *Abba*? It was his abiding sense of communion with the Father, his knowing he was never alone. That which Jesus felt with his Father was the same companionship his disciples, and all Christians, came to feel with him. This is movingly portrayed in the Emmaus narrative, wherein Cleopas and his companion had the comfort of his fellowship, when "Jesus himself came near and went with them"– when he, unknown to them, walked along beside them and then "went in to stay with them" at eventide (Luke 24:13-35). There, as they broke bread together, they came to recognize their Lord, the one whom they had been given as their Friend. They had opened their door to him, and he came in to sup with them and they with him (see Rev 3:20). He vanished from their sight, but their eyes had been opened—to know he was with them always, and that this itself would be their prayer.

The basis, the source of prayer is faith—and the faith is faith in Jesus. It is the believing that is not afraid to ask, because this he wants: "Ask, and it will be given you; search, and you will find; knock, and the door will be opened for you" (Luke 11:9), for who would give his child a snake if he asked for food, and will not the heavenly Father even more give to his children the good things of their asking (see 11:11-13). After all, he does know what we need before we ask him (see Matt 56:8).

We recall again the road to Emmaus: Jesus drew near and went with his disciples. He continued with them and then "walked ahead as if he were going on" until they stopped and invited him, "Stay with us because it is almost evening and the day is now almost over" (Luke 24:28-29). They asked him, and so he answered: He went in to stay with them, he became known to them in the breaking of bread, and he opened their eyes. "Stay with us": This, at heart, is the recurrent prayer of the Bible, the longing of the psalmist who wanted to dwell in the Lord's house all the days of his life. "Stay with us": it is the prayer answered by our believing, "I am with you always...."

THE CHRISTIAN LACK

We have looked above to the lament, so prevalent in the Old Testament. Lament has not become part of Christian prayer. And that is a pity. There is the fact, of course, that the Psalter is prominent in Christian worship. Psalms of lament figure largely. The truth is: They are not acknowledged as such. The Christian who, formally, prays a psalm of lament is, rarely if ever, directing a passionate complaint to God—much less at God! It is precisely as uninhibited complaint that lament functions. We Christians simply miss the point.

A depreciatory attitude towards the lament reflects the fact that lamentation has been severed from prayer in Christian piety throughout the history of the church. In the Old Testament lamentation is an intrinsic component of prayer, as is shown in the Psalter, with its high percentage of psalms of lamentation. In the Christian church, on the other hand, the lament no longer receives a hearing. This transformation took place without being discussed in the official theologies of the church. Nowhere is there a reasoned rejection of lamentation as an intrinsic component of prayer; the severing of lamentation from prayer took place without comment.[36]

Perhaps it might be said that confession of sin has become the Christianized form of lament. Both in Christian theology and Christian worship suffering has receded into the background. It is stressed that Jesus Christ's work of salvation has to do with forgiveness of sin and eternal life. There is much less concern with the gospel witness to Jesus' total sensitivity toward human suffering. The result is that the "sufferings of this world" are regarded as of little importance. Sin is what really matters. The believing Christian will not complain but will "offer up" one's sufferings. It is something Jesus did not do! — Gethsemane and the cross! Indeed one may get the impression that though Jesus of Nazareth cared for those who suffered and pitied those who mourned, the risen Lord is preoccupied solely with sin. Claus Westermann has put it aptly:

> There is no passage in the Gospels which suggest that Jesus saw his task to be one of convincing the sufferer that one must bear suffering patiently. There are narratives in which Jesus combines the forgiveness of sins with healing, but there are no narratives in which Jesus puts the forgiveness of sins in the place of healing.[37]

While the New Testament in no way prevents the Christian from lamenting, in practice the lament has been excluded in Christian relationship with God and has virtually disappeared from prayer and worship. This exclusion does not come from the New Testament. It is surely due to Greek influence: the Greek notion of God and the ethic of Stoicism. The Hebrew God is one who welcomes dialogue and invites plain speaking. Israel obliged! We have seen that Israel could dare to complain to God of God, could talk back at God without restraint. It is an approach

91

endorsed by Jesus himself. He acknowledged that sufferers have the right to lament their suffering. His Father is One who is moved to compassion by the laments of those who suffer.

We live in a world that has more than its measure of pain. Israel did not suffer stoically but cried out to a God who could relieve pain. Here is a lesson we Christians could profitably take to heart. We live in a world of sin; we are sinners among sinners. We need to acknowledge our sinfulness. Again, Israel points the way of candid confession of sin and of total trust in God's boundless mercy. And here, too, is a lesson. Those who pray in repentance do not grovel, but maintain quiet dignity. Prayer must always be worthy of the God who is addressed and of the people of God who pray.

The Eucharist

Apart from two passages in 1 Corinthians it might have seemed that Paul knew nothing of the Eucharist—surely a salutary reminder that what we have from Paul are occasional letters by no means giving his whole theology or the full content of his preaching. At any rate, 1 Corinthians 11:23–26 puts beyond doubt that the Lord's Supper had been part of Christian faith and practice from the start. This passage is the earliest reference in the New Testament to the Eucharist:

> For I have received from the Lord what I also handed on to you, that the Lord Jesus on the night when he was betrayed took a loaf of bread, and when he had given thanks, he broke it and said, "This is my body that is for you. Do this in remembrance of me." In the same way he took the cup also, after supper, saying, "This cup is the new covenant in my blood. Do this, as often as you drink it, in remembrance of me." For as often as you eat this bread and drink the cup, you proclaim the Lord's death until he comes.

Paul solemnly passes on a tradition which, because it reached him through an authentically Christian community, had come to him from "the Lord." In fact, he is citing an established liturgical text—likely the usage of the church of Antioch. He reminds the Corinthians of this tradition in the course of correcting an abuse in their celebration (11:17-22). The striking point in the passage (11:23-26) is that Paul does not think of the Eucharist and Christ's presence through it in a static manner as might be suggested by the formulas, "This is...." Instead, the account is full of dynamic expressions. It is no mere making present of Christ's body and blood; it is a proclamation, and a memorial, of his death, of an event. Similarly, the cup is "the new covenant in my blood," that is, an event, the making of a covenant that has lasting and definitive consequences for the life of the people who are included in the covenant.

The command to repeat the action of the Lord, "Do this...," not only binds the community to celebrate the Lord's Supper regularly and thus keep alive the meaning of the death of Jesus, but places upon it the obligation to proclaim the redemptive meaning of his death. "Do this in remembrance of me": Paul wants to evoke an active remembrance that would make the past present by recall of total commitment to Christ. Significantly, the "proclamation" of the Lord's death is in terms of an eating and drinking that implies a true communion—for nothing but love, expressed in warm table fellowship, can continue to proclaim the meaning of the death of Christ.

Just here was the Corinthian problem. The Eucharist was celebrated in the setting of a meal. At Corinth it had become fashionable for the better-off members of the community to gather beforehand and dine well on their lavish provisions of food and drink. Later, when the workers and slaves turned up, the Eucharist was celebrated (11:17-22, 33-34). In Paul's eyes this was not only a glaring abuse but a perversion of the whole meaning and purpose of the Lord's Supper. He had declared: "The cup of blessing that we bless, is it not a sharing in the blood of Christ? The bread that we break, is it not a sharing in the body of Christ?" (10:16). His emphasis was not just on the one bread and the one cup but on the *sharing* of the one bread and the one cup. It is because, in sharing mode, they partake of the one bread that the celebrants become "one body"—the Body of Christ: "Because there is one bread, we who are many are one body, for we all partake of the one bread" (10:17). The Eucharist was meant to be a bond of unity; in Corinth it had been turned into a wedge between the haves and the have-nots. No wonder Paul does not commend the Corinthian practice (11:17,22).

Because this context is ignored, verse 29 has been regularly misinterpreted—"For all who eat and drink without discerning the body, eat and drink judgment against themselves." Traditionally, the verse has been urged in support of the doctrine of the "real presence"—the sin is that one fails to distinguish the Eucharist from ordinary food and drink. In point of fact, the "real presence" is not an issue; the Corinthians do believe that they are eating and drinking "the body and blood of the Lord" (11:27). The point at issue is that what was designed to unify is being used to divide. The "body" in question in verse 29 is *the body of the community*. The Corinthian celebration is not communion. The sacrament of the body and blood of the Lord is being abused to rend the body of Christ.

Paul goes further: "When you come together, it is not really to eat the Lord's Supper" (11:20). A Lord's Supper that was not a shared supper, that was not a *sharing* in the one bread and in the one cup was not *in fact* the Lord's Supper. Even though the ritual words (vv. 24–25) were said, the lack of love (vv. 21–22) meant that in reality there was no Eucharist. The essence of Paul's reaction is that there can be no Eucharist in a community whose members do not love one another. This must surely give food for thought. To what extent is our Mass truly celebration of the Lord's Supper? Salutary indeed—but one would strike a more positive note.

The Book of Revelation is markedly liturgical. It is explicitly designated for reading in a liturgy (1:3), very likely a eucharistic liturgy. It closes with a look to the One who is coming soon, "bringing his reward with him" (22:12). He was the One who had conquered by laying down his life. These Christians, if they were faithful, would share his triumph. They look to his coming. In the meantime, as they celebrate their Eucharist, they have his presence with them. They have the reminder of his victory and the assurance of his promise: "As often as you eat this bread and drink the cup, you proclaim the Lord's death until he comes" (1 Cor 11:26). They do not have to wait, bereft, for his final coming. Yet, they long. "My desire is to depart and be with Christ, for that is far better" (Phil 1:23). It is in their going to him that the Lord will come to them—and to us! *Marana tha.* Come, Lord Jesus! Perhaps in our eucharistic celebration we might capture something of this assurance and this hope.

ANSWERING THE CALL TO DISCIPLESHIP

Within the broad Christian vocation, some are called to special service: ministry, religious life. A call to serve is, surely, privilege. Response is not in an initial assent but in faithful service. One recalls the parable of the two sons (Matt 21:28-31). From one a prompt "I go, sir"—but he did not go. From the other an initial "I will not"—later, he changed his mind and went. We may presume that his response was constant.

Constancy is not the only requirement. There is, too, the kind and quality of the response. There will, often enough, be the temptation that "doing one's thing" is right and proper, even when other factors point to a different priority. There is need for discernment here. Initiative is to be welcomed. Experience shows that individuals have, time and again, launched a work or a movement that has borne great fruit. One thinks of the founders of religious orders and congregations. There is a place for magnanimity and for an understanding that has a touch of humor. One recalls the wry observation of a religious superior: The trouble with holy people is—they are very stubborn!

If service is the answer to call, it is, too, the answer to the scandal of vocation—why one is called rather than another. The call is not for oneself but for others. It is a charism, and, as Paul has firmly shown, the very raison d'etre of charism is the building-up of the Christian community. Another thing, response is the service we are able to render at any one time. There may be obstacles beyond our control—not least the realities of illness and age. It is wise to listen to Milton: "They also serve, who only stand and wait." A feature of the richness of Christianity is that there is no one way of being Christian. There are, indeed, basic, essential factors; beyond those, there is place for broad variety.

As Jesus passed along by the Sea of Galilee, he saw Simon and his brother Andrew casting a net into the sea—for they were fishermen. And Jesus said to them, "Follow me and I will make you fish for people." And immediately they left their nets and followed him. As he went on a little farther, he saw James son of Zebedee and his brother John, who were in their boat mending the nets. Immediately he called them; and they left their father Zebedee in the boat with the hired men, and followed him. (Mark 1:16–20)

This passage, with two parallel episodes (1:19–20; 2:13–14), was shaped by Mark to bring out the nature of Jesus' call and the nature of the Christian response; in short, to show what "following Jesus" means. We are shown that the sovereign call of Jesus evokes the response of those called, a free response as we learn in the episode of the one who could not bring himself to follow—the man "who had great possessions" (10:17–22). These fishermen leave all, nets, boat and father, to follow Jesus without hesitation. The decisive factor is the person of Jesus himself. In order to become a disciple of Jesus one does not need to be exceptional. What counts is not intellectual or moral aptitude but the gracious call of Jesus. It is the mighty, immediate impression of Jesus on Peter and his companions, reinforced by his personal word of call, that brought them into his following and made them his disciples. The whole episode is stylized, of course. Mark is not intent on describing a scene from the ministry of Jesus. Rather, he is concerned with the theological dimension of a typical call to discipleship.

In Mark 1:17 the verb *akolouthein*, "to follow," is a technical term for discipleship. Frequent throughout Mark's gospel, a significant occurrence is in 15:40–41:

There were also women looking on from afar, among whom were Mary Magdalene, and Mary the mother of James the younger and of Joses, and Salome, who, when he was in Galilee, followed him, and ministered to him; and also many other women who came up with him to Jerusalem.

These Galilean women had followed Jesus: They are disciples. This alerts us to the fact that, throughout the Gospels, "disciple" must be taken in an inclusive sense: The Jesus movement included men and women. It was another blow by Jesus for equality in human relationships. A mixed itinerant group of men and women would have been glaringly unconventional in his first-century Jewish Palestinian setting. Jesus was no respecter of persons, as his opponents wryly acknowledged (Mark 12:14). He, consistently, upheld the dignity of women. Jesus has, by his alleged followers, been betrayed in so many ways, most shamefully, perhaps, in the attitude toward and treatment of women by the Christian churches, down to our day.

DISCIPLESHIP

Christians may be children of God but they are truly such only on condition that they understand what it means and live with its demands. Mark's own understanding of discipleship was the same as that of Paul: "If children, then heirs, heirs of God and joint heirs with Christ—if, in fact, we suffer with him so that we may also be glorified with him" (Rom 8:17). His preoccupation with discipleship follows hard on his concern with Christology. The way of discipleship had been firmly traced by Jesus himself. "If any want to become my followers, let them deny themselves and take up their cross and follow me" (8:34). For Mark there is no other way of discipleship. Following the path of the victory of Christ, the Christian is not preserved from suffering and even death, but is sustained through suffering and death.

Coming directly after the first prediction of the passion (Mark 8:31-33), the passage 8:34-9:1 asserts, unequivocally, that the disciples of the Son of Man (v. 31) must necessarily walk in his path. Jesus had "called the crowd with his disciples" (v. 34): This challenge was addressed to all. The loyal disciple would not be preoccupied with personal interests but would follow in sustained faithfulness to Jesus. The way of discipleship is not easy, and one may be tempted to shrink from what it entails. To seek thus to evade risk and save one's life—to have things one's own way—would be to suffer the loss of one's true self. One prepared and willing to risk all for Jesus and for the good news is one who will achieve authentic selfhood. If human life on earth is so much more precious than anything else in creation, if no one can put a price on it, how much more precious the eternal life to be won by the faithful disciple. There is challenge. A warning sounds for one who would not follow, for one who would draw back, ashamed of the Way, one who would seek to save one's life (see 4:14-19). Jesus, too, the warning rings, will be ashamed of such a one, will not acknowledge such a one when he will reappear in glory at the end (8:38). And his return will not be long delayed. Already, in this generation, God's reign will be manifest in power. It is impossible for us to gauge what such conviction meant for Mark and his community. What is undeniable is that Mark was still certain that a Christian had to come to terms with the cross. Once this had been grasped, one had to spread the good news (see 13:10).

Mark assuredly looked beyond the ministry of Jesus. Like the author of Revelation, his concern was for the persecuted community of his day (see Mark 13:9-13)—though in neither case was it yet all-out persecution. He reminded those followers of a rejected and crucified Messiah that it should not surprise that they, too, were called upon to suffer. The cross had turned the values of the world upside down—it is indeed "a stumbling-block" and "foolishness" (see 1 Cor 1:23). They must be steadfast in face of persecution. They must not be ashamed of Jesus' way of humiliation and suffering and death if they do not want the glorious Son of Man to be ashamed of them at his coming. And they hear his comforting assurance, "Surely, I am coming soon" (Rev 22:20; see Mark 9:1).

The second prediction of the passion (Mark 9:30-32) is followed by further instruction on discipleship. It was needed because in verses 33 through 34 the disciples' lack of understanding is blatant. They, disciples of a master so soon to suffer bitter humiliation and death are all too humanly involved in petty squabbling over precedence. The Teacher took his seat and called the Twelve to him. His message was unequivocal: "Whoever wants to be first must be last of all and servant of all" (v. 35). He backed up his word with a prophetic gesture: the presentation of a little child. The manner of it tells much of the delicate sensitivity of Jesus—"taking it in his arms"—a touch proper to Mark (see 10:16). "Whoever welcomes one such child in my name welcomes me..." (v. 37). "Welcome" means loving service of the weaker members of the community, those who stand in greatest need of being served. A Christian is one baptized "into the name of" Jesus (Matt 28:19; 1 Cor 1:13,15), so becoming his. That is why one meets (serves) Christ himself in the disciple and meets the Father in Christ. This is the dignity of Christian service. Mark has made the point that the revelation of Jesus cannot be acknowledged by one who is not ready to enter into the spirit of discipleship and thereby become "last" and "servant." One would hope that the Christian of today is attuned to the unambiguous message of this word of Jesus: Greatness in his church is found in *diakonia,* service, and only there. A first step is to have discerned this. It is the right of the people of God to have such service. It is their right to demand that leadership in the Church, at every level, be service, not in word but in deed.

Paul

It would be surprising indeed if we might not learn something of discipleship from one who is, arguably, the greatest Christian of all: the apostle Paul. We are familiar with the story of the encounter on the road to Damascus (Acts 9:1–19; 22:5–16; 26:10–18; see Gal 1:12–17). It would seem that the embracing of the Christian Way by the committed Pharisee Saul, erstwhile persecutor of this "perfidious" sect, was instantaneous. In a sense, this is so. Saul was changed. But he himself has told us that, after the traumatic experience, he needed time for it to sink in. He has put it like this:

> You have heard, no doubt, of my earlier life in Judaism. I was violently persecuting the church of God and was trying to destroy it. I advanced in Judaism beyond many among my people of the same age, for I was far more zealous for the traditions of my ancestors. But when God, who had set me apart before I was born and called me through his grace, was pleased to reveal his Son to me, so that I might proclaim him among the Gentiles, I did not confer with a single person, nor did I go up to Jerusalem to those who were apostles

before me, but I went away at once into Arabia, and afterwards I returned to Damascus. (Gal 1:13-17)

The purpose of Paul's withdrawal to "Arabia" (more or less modern Jordan) is not clear. Because he was so sure that the revelation of the risen Lord involved his call to be apostle to the Gentiles, he must have, very soon, become involved in missionary activity among the Nabateans ("Arabia"). But he surely must have needed time to come to terms with a radical shock to his whole religious commitment until then. Up to the moment of the Damascus encounter he had had no doubt at all of where he stood: He was a Law-observant Jew and very proud of it.

> Circumcised on the eighth day, a member of the people of Israel, of the tribe of Benjamin, a Hebrew born of Hebrews; as to the law a Pharisee, as to zeal a persecutor of the church, as to righteousness under the law blameless. (Phil 3:5-6)

Paul, writing twenty years or more after the Damascus experience, does not, in the least, apologize for his past. He is quite sure that, then, he had lived up to his convictions and had followed his conscience. It is this that underlines his further declaration:

> Yet whatever gains I had, these I have come to regard as loss because of Christ. More than that, I regard everything as loss because of the surpassing value of knowing Christ Jesus my Lord. (3:7-8)

In dealing with Paul one has to realize that one is faced with a character of sheer integrity. Saul the Pharisee was perceptively aware of the threat posed by the Christian movement to his understanding of Judaism. He reacted with typical honesty and ardor. When the great change came, it was not, in any sense, our conventional "conversion." In the first place, there was not yet another religion to convert to. Christianity became a religion distinct from Judaism after A.D. 70. What had happened is that Paul the Jew had come to acknowledge that other Jew, Jesus of Nazareth, as the Messiah of Jewish expectation. As disciple of the Messiah he was not turning his back on Judaism; he was entering into its fullness.

Paul, the Jew, had come to view his past in a new light; he had now really found his way. He was now, and to the end, an apostle: "called to be an apostle of Christ Jesus by the will of God" (1 Cor 1:1), "set apart for the gospel of God" (Rom 1:1), indeed, "sent neither by human commission nor from human authorities, but through Jesus Christ and God the Father" (Gal 1:1). He is not and cannot be "ashamed" of that Gospel. He is convinced that the "gospel" is the "power of God": it is not a philosophy nor a religious system—nor even a message. It is power; but "power," in Paul's paradoxical view, is nothing other than the "word of the cross" (1 Cor 1:18). That power comes in response to faith: saying yes to God, letting God be God for us. It is through Jesus Christ that God makes his claim. He is our God "who did not withhold his own Son but gave him up for all of us" (Rom 8:32).

PILGRIMAGE

The pilgrimage of Paul the apostle was, literally, a journey of sweat and blood. Paul was the first great *peregrinus pro Christo* (pilgrim for Christ)—as the Irish missionary monks liked to call themselves. The personal cost to Paul of his missionary endeavor was enormous. Most painful was the fierce antagonism of some of his Jewish-Christian fellow workers. It was just such opposition that wrenched from him an impassioned listing of his trials:

> Are they ministers of Christ? I am a better one: with far greater labors, far more imprisonments, with countless floggings, and often near death. Five times I have received from the Jews the forty lashes minus one. Three times I was beaten with rods. Once I received a stoning. Three times I was shipwrecked; for a night and a day I was adrift at sea; on frequent journeys, in danger from rivers, danger from bandits, danger from my own people, danger from Gentiles, danger in the city, danger in the wilderness, danger at sea, danger from false brothers and sisters; in toil and hardship, through many a sleepless night, hungry and thirsty, often without food, cold and naked. And, besides other things, I am under daily pressure because of my anxiety for all the churches. (2 Cor 11:23–28)

An impressive catalog indeed. Yet his last trial had to be the most painful of all: the frustration of his plans, the abrupt ending of his missionary activity. He had written, confidently, to the Romans:

> I hope to see you in passing as I go to Spain, and to be sped on my journey there by you, once I have enjoyed your company for a little. At present, however, I am going to Jerusalem with aid for the saints....When therefore I have completed this, and have delivered to them what has been raised, I shall go on by way of you to Spain. (Rom 15:24–25,28)

No reading between the lines here. Paul is straightforward and to the point. Because, for Luke (in Acts), Paul's goal has to be Rome, there is no reason to question the broad lines of his account of how Paul did get there. Paul's planned visit to Jerusalem turned out badly. He fell victim of Jewish outrage against an alleged traitor to Judaism. Whisked, for his own safety, to the Caesarea headquarters of the Roman procurator, he languished in prison for two years during the office of Antonius Felix. When the new procurator, Porcius Festus, briefed by the Jewish leaders, wanted him to stand trial in Jerusalem, Paul, as a Roman citizen, appealed to the imperial tribunal. He did reach Rome, but as a prisoner, to spend two years under house arrest (Acts 21:27–28:16). And there he met his death.

We do not know if Paul's ambitious plan for a journey to Spain took shape. As likely as not, here too he was frustrated. He had found from experience that his own words were more true than he had realized when he wrote them: "For God's foolishness is wiser than human wisdom, and God's weakness is stronger than human strength" (1 Cor 1:25). Is God, then, a God who toys with his most faithful servants? The stories of Jeremiah and Paul would suggest as much. What is the point of a pilgrimage that ends in failure? The answer is that God is on the side of the losers, not the winners. And, surely, it is more heroic, having striven to the full, to wend one's way to a goal marked "Failure" than to stride to the winner's podium. The real question, of course, is: What is success—or failure? The question, fully answered by Jesus, has been well answered by Paul.

One does not need to spell out the lessons of Paul's life and words—but we can make a few points. We learn from him that the cross is a central factor in the Christian way of life, making sense of the otherwise meaningless realities of suffering and death. We learn that, however generously we give ourselves to the task or tasks set out for us, the harvest is never ours, but is always the Lord's (see 1 Cor 3:5-9). This should give us serene confidence. And, when we find that our work for God is blocked by one obstacle or another—a seemingly unintelligible directive, some unexpected opposition, ill-health—and we know discouragement, then we can think of the trials of Paul and his frustration. Perhaps in that thought we will find comfort.

ANSWERING THE CALL TO PROPHECY

If one believes that the prophetic voice is an essential Christian voice, a voice surely needed in our day, one should have, in the first place, a proper understanding of prophecy. Here, surely, a look at the prophets of Israel will help. What we find will stand as challenge. Prophets are not comfortable people. They point the accusing finger. They speak disturbing truth. Often their truth is found in a radical questioning of our ready assumptions. They are a threat, and a threat must be contained. The result: a suffering prophet. But there is no silencing the prophetic voice. It speaks, surer than ever, beyond the suffering and death of the prophet.

Thus Says Yahweh

A biblical prophet is a spokesman, a herald, called to speak in the name of God. (One, here, departs from inclusive language. The fact is that, though there were women prophets, the recorded prophets of Israel were, all of them, men.) We must, here, beware of taking the words *prophet* and *prophecy* after their common usage in everyday English—a prophet being one who "predicts" and the verb meaning "to foretell." The biblical prophets did, indeed, look to the future, but to a limited extent, and almost always they looked to the immediate future. They were more concerned with the present and often just as much concerned with the past.

The typical Israelite prophet is one who has received a divine call to be a messenger and interpreter of the Word of God. He is one who has met God. The Word that has come to him compels him to speak. "The Lord has spoken, who can but prophesy?" asks Amos (3:8). Jeremiah, despondent because of his unrelieved message of woe to the people he loves, would stifle the Word: "If I say, 'I will not mention him, or speak any more in his name, then within me there is something like a burning fire shut up in my bones; I am weary with holding it in, and I cannot'" (Jer 20:9). Whatever the form of the message, the prophet's vision of God had permeated the manner of his thought so that he saw things from God's point of view and was convinced that he so saw them.

This perhaps helps to explain the true dimension of the phrase *koh amar Yahweh*—"thus says Yahweh"—which so often opens or closes the prophetic oracle. It does not, each time it occurs, imply direct revelation. Rather, one should recognize in the formula the normal development of an initial vocation. Armed with this conviction, the prophet was outspoken, a fearless critic of the people and of the establishment. Each of the great prophets richly deserved the epithet petulantly branded by Ahab on Elijah: "troubler of Israel" (1 Kgs 18:17). The prophet's message is always primarily to his contemporaries. He is a preacher who addresses the people of his own generation. He does so even when he announces the future. The prophet claimed to speak in the name of God; this claim is explicit in the formula *koh amar Yahweh*. But the phrase alone is not sufficient to authenticate the message, for those whom we call "false prophets" could and did declare, "Thus says Yahweh." Jeremiah 28 is illuminating on this score. Jeremiah's rival is called a *nabi* (prophet). He spoke in the name of God (28:2), and yet his words were not true. The hearers of Hananiah and Jeremiah, however, could not discriminate between them merely from their words and prophetic gestures. Hence, Jeremiah offers two criteria: (1) the fulfillment of his prediction—where prediction is in question (28:16-17); (2) the conformity of his teaching to traditional doctrine (28:7-8)—what we might call the "analogy of faith." Deuteronomy gives these same criteria: the fulfillment of prophecy (Deut 18:21-22) and the more important one of the doctrine and life of the prophet (13:1-5), which should be in the line of pure Yahwism, should be in harmony with the moral will of God. It must always have been extremely difficult for people to distinguish between prophet and prophet.

Suffering Prophet

An inescapable feature of true prophetic experience is suffering. It looms largely in the life of all the great prophets, its form as varied as human experience. In every case, however, it took the shape of the rejection of the prophetic word. There is also a more personal suffering. The tragic marital experience of Hosea was the inspiration, and the strength, of his prophetic message—significantly, his message of hope. The sudden death of Ezekiel's wife was turned into a prophetic sign. There is something very poignant here. "Son of man, with one blow I am about to take away from you the delight of your eyes; yet you shall not mourn or weep, nor shall your tears run down....So I spoke to the people in the morning, and at evening my wife died" (Ezek 24:16,18). "Thus Ezekiel shall be a sign to you" (v. 24): as warning of the impending doom of Jerusalem—but at what a personal cost to the prophet. And Jeremiah: "I did not sit in the company of merrymakers, nor did I rejoice; under the weight of your hand I sat alone" (Jer 15:17).

What one wishes to look at, more specifically, is how a prophet's life was reflective of divine suffering. Biblical metaphor demands that we acknowledge a God who grieves and laments and suffers. A suffering God? To speak of God as one who suffers is to speak in metaphor, or analogically. God suffers—but not in the manner that humans suffer. There is always in the metaphor a large element that is discontinuous with the reality that is God. And analogy means that, though we may assert that God suffers, we cannot know at all what divine suffering is. Still, if one is to take seriously biblical language and imagery, one must acknowledge a God who suffers and mourns. Greek notions of divine impassibility, ideas alien to biblical thought, must not be allowed to obscure that comforting truth.

God suffers because of his people's rejection of him; he is deeply wounded by the broken relationship. His steadfast will endures as he bears with the human party. He is not legalistic, never vindictive; he seeks salvation, not judgment, life, not death. His extraordinary patience takes him to unexpected lengths in his striving to heal the breached relationship. God suffers with the suffering people. He becomes a mourner—a God in sackcloth and ashes. For God to mourn with the mourning means not only divine compassion; it means that mourning must one day cease. God mourns because Israel has died, but death is the way to rebirth. God mourns over non-Israelite peoples, weeps for the sufferers of the world. The tears of God are seed of new life. God suffers for the people. Because God is not a legalist, he chooses to bear the people's sins. He is wearied by the burden of their sin. By assuming that burden he gives them room to breathe and raises them from death.[38]

When we look at the prophets—and one may reasonably generalize from Jeremiah—we can see that the prophets were rejected as much as God. They suffered because of being rejected. They suffered with the people. They suffered for the people. The Suffering Servant, a prophetic figure in the Moses-Jeremiah-Ezekiel mold, is reflective of the suffering of God: "Surely he has borne our griefs and carried our sorrows" (Isa 53:4). We may maintain: A prophet's life reflects the divine life. If to hear the word of a prophet is to hear God, to see a prophet is to see the Word of God enfleshed. A prophet not only speaks the Word of God, he embodies it. And the prophet suffers precisely as servant of God.

The Prophet Jesus

If prophecy seems to have ceased in the last centuries of the Old Testament era, it emerged again, dramatically, in the person of John the Baptist. And the evidence would suggest that Jesus of Nazareth began his mission as disciple of the Baptist and remained so until the arrest of John. Although he admired John, Jesus was to follow his own way. John was a prophet of doom who preached "a baptism of repentance for the forgiveness of sins" (Mark 1:4). Jesus proclaimed: "The kingdom of God is at hand" (1:15). Where John prophesied the judgment of God, Jesus prophesied the salvation of God. Hearing, in prison, of the activity of Jesus, a perplexed John sent two of his disciples to investigate.

Jesus' reply was: "Go and tell John what you have seen and heard: the blind receive their sight, the lame walk, the lepers are cleansed, the deaf hear, the dead are raised, the poor have good news brought to them" (Luke 7:22). One can read between the lines. John is being told that there is another prophetic message, another prophetic style. One might put it: John is being told that if he is an Amos, Jesus is a Hosea. The concluding word—"And blessed is anyone who takes no offense at me" (7:23)—is Jesus' gentle plea for the openness and understanding of his master.

In the Gospels Jesus refers to himself as a prophet, if only indirectly. Notably, his reference is in a context of rejection (see Mark 6:4; Luke 4:24; 13:33–35). It is reasonable to maintain that he saw himself as an eschatological prophet: the prophet of the end-time. He was the one empowered by God's Spirit to proclaim to Israel God's definitive call to conversion and deliverance. Jewish piety of the time had come to view the prophets as rejected figures and often as martyrs (see Matt 23:35). Hence, Jesus' implicit assumption of a prophetic role already pointed to his probable fate. And, if the suffering prophets spoke of the suffering of God, how much more faithfully the suffering of Jesus mirrored the suffering of his *Abba*.

Christian Prophecy

One must recall that the first Christians were exclusively Jews. With their background, they took prophecy for granted and accepted, without difficulty, that Jesus was a prophet (while much more than a prophet). Naturally, prophecy was a feature of early Christianity. Jewish Christians, heirs of a tradition of prophets who spoke confidently in the name of Yahweh—*koh amar Yahweh*—had no problem in speaking, confidently, in the name of the Lord Jesus. In our Gospels some of the sayings attributed to Jesus are, in fact, words of Christian prophets. In Revelation 2–3 the messages to the seven churches, from the Lord of the churches, are mediated through the prophet John. And the Acts of the Apostles makes abundantly clear that prophets were active in the early Church (see Acts 11:27–28; 13:1–2; 15:32; 21:8–9,11).

Luke, indeed, shows us, in striking fashion, prophecy in action. At Antioch, while the brothers and sisters "were worshiping the Lord and fasting, the Holy Spirit said, 'Set apart for me Barnabas and Saul for the work to which I have called them'" (Acts 13:2). Just before is a listing of "prophets and teachers" (13:1). Doubtless, this call of the Spirit came by the word of a prophet. The Antioch community had come to believe that the time was ripe for a full-blown mission to the Gentiles. They prayed about it. A Christian prophet assured them that this mission was, indeed, the will of God—and went on to designate the missionaries who would implement the plan of the community.

Paul helps us to understand what is meant by prophecy. In general the emergence of New Testament prophets might be said to constitute a true awakening of Old Testament-style prophetism. Paul lets us have an idea of its nature and scope. In 1 Thessalonians 5:19 he urges: "Do not quench the Spirit, do not despise prophesying." Prophecy is not to be despised because it is nothing short of word of the Spirit spoken through the prophet to the Church. The prophet is one who "speaks to people for their upbuilding and encouragement and consolation"; he is one who "builds up the church" (1 Cor 14:3-4). Indeed, throughout 1 Cor 12–14 Paul is responding to a Corinthian question: Which is the highest charism? Or, more precisely, the question seems to have been whether prophecy or tongue-speaking is the higher gift. While Paul is not content to settle the matter on this level, to set off one against the other, and instead broadens the issue, there is no doubt as to his high estimation of prophecy.

Early Christians believed that the ultimate revelation had come in the person and teaching of Jesus. Prophecy was a teaching function. It was confident and forceful preaching. A passage in Acts is quite revealing. We find the Jerusalem community in thanksgiving prayer after Peter and John had been released from arrest and interrogation. They pray: "And now, Lord, look at their threats, and grant to your servants to speak your word with all boldness..." (4:29). Their prayer was answered: "They were all filled with the Holy Spirit and spoke the word of God with boldness" (4:31). "To speak the word of God with boldness" is, it seems to me, an apt definition of prophecy.

Our glance at the early Church hardly suggests that prophecy was a temporary expedient. An older apologetic did, incredibly, maintain that such was the case. Once we had in place an established institutional authority, that primitive prop was no longer needed! In fact, the prophetic voice—though it may not have been named as such nor recognized as such—has never been silent. Predictably, it has been consistently muzzled. Today we are more discerning or, perhaps, less coy. We can speak of prophets again. We speak even of a prophetic role for the Church in our society. Today as much as ever—more than ever?—we need our prophets. As ever, they make us feel uncomfortable; as ever, they are misunderstood; as ever, they are rejected. They are critics of our world, and of the Church—that is their role And who will seriously argue that world and Church are not open to criticism?

We have observed that suffering is a consistent ingredient of the prophetic role. A main feature of that pain is unconcern for the Word—sheer apathy. That is bad enough. Surely a much deeper pain is opposition on the part of those from whom the prophet might have expected support. It seems to be almost a rule that the voice of the prophet is heard only when it is stilled in death. The prophetic theologians of Vatican II are the rare exceptions; they were heard and vindicated in their lifetime. The pattern has resumed: Their successors are under a cloud. These can take hope that their striving is not in vain. They are in goodly company.

The prophetic call is costly. Response demands sterling faith and mighty courage:

> The prophet has the courage, literally, of his or her convictions. If we do not call society to account in the name of God, who will? If we see disaster coming, we should have the courage to say so because we know that, as Peter said to the high priest, we must obey God rather than men, and because we know that—perhaps even beyond judgment—God's last word is good news.[39]

Such is, or should be, the prophetic role of the Church. History shows that an institution as such cannot speak with a compelling prophetic voice. As in Israel, as with the Baptist and Jesus, as in the early Church and through the eras of the Church, we need our prophets. The Spirit takes care that they are with us. We are not very hospitable. We want them to go away and leave us in peace—those "troublers of Israel." The day will come when we will bless them. All the while, of course, we ignore or confront them! Thank God, there are always those brave women and men who do hear and heed the call of the Spirit. It is a lonely and a costly way. It is a needed call because the prophetic voice is voice of the Spirit to the churches (see Rev 2-3, passim).

To be a witness to Christ is a lifelong task. To be a prophet, Christ's spokesperson, is a challenging task. There is, indeed, the privilege of service, but the cost is high. Every person who strives to preach and teach the Word of God knows at once fulfillment and frustration. There is no more worthwhile service. But one must feel the pain that ripples through the pages of the New Testament, the pain of preachers of the good news: The word is not heeded.

6. *Steadfast Anchor of the Soul*

Hope

We have this hope, a sure and steadfast anchor of the soul.
(Heb 6:19)

THE RULE OF GOD

Now after John was arrested [delivered up] Jesus came to Galilee, proclaiming the good news of God, and saying, "The time is fulfilled, and the kingdom of God has come near; repent, and believe in the good news." (Mark 1:14-15)

esus is here firmly cast as a prophet, issuing a challenge and an invitation. He had a burning concern for the renewal of the people of Israel as God's holy elect. He would not define the holiness of God's people in cultic terms. He redefined it in terms of wholeness. Where other contemporary Jewish movements were, in their various ways, exclusive, the Jesus movement was inclusive. His challenge and his invitation were to all. What Jesus claimed was that the divine intervention of God expected for the end-time was, in some sort, happening in his ministry. The kingdom is here and now present in history in that the power of evil is broken, sins are forgiven, sinners are gathered into God's friendship. The kingdom, though in its fullness still in the future, comes as present offer, in actual gift, through the proclamation of the good news. But it arrives only on condition of the positive response of the hearer.

The Reign of God

The precise phrase "kingdom of God" occurs only once in the Old Testament, in Wisdom 10:10. The expression was not current in Judaism at the time of Jesus and was not widely used by early

111

Christians. "Kingdom of God" is found predominantly in the Synoptic Gospels and then almost always on the lips of Jesus. It was evidently central to Jesus' proclamation. It was his way of speaking of God himself coming in power to manifest his definitive rule in the end-time. This is why "reign" or "rule" of God is a more satisfactory rendering of the Aramaic *malkutha di elaha*, which would have been Jesus' term. Jesus preached the kingdom: He preached that God is the ultimate meaning of this world. The rule of God does not signify something "spiritual," outside of this world; it is not "pie in the sky." Jesus was supremely concerned with our real world. He spoke so vaguely of the future that the first Christians could expect that the end would come in their day (see Mark 9:1; 13:20). When he preached the kingdom of God, he envisaged a revolution in the existing order. He made two fundamental demands: He asked for personal conversion and he postulated a restructuring of the human world. Conversion *(metanoia)* meant changing one's mode of thinking and acting to suit God's purpose for humankind. It would be a new manner of existing before God.

But conversion also meant a turning from the established order. Jesus made the point, so clearly grasped and effectively developed by Paul, that it is not law that saves—not even the Law—it is love. Jesus' outlook and conduct were marked by freedom. His understanding of freedom is again faithfully reflected by Paul: freedom to serve. Jesus did not make life easier. His disconcerting word was that love knows no limits. He proclaimed not law but good news. The Gospel is good news for one who can grasp its spirit and react positively to it. His good news embraced basic equality: All men and women, as children of the Father, are brothers and sisters. Good news so understood is a radical challenge to all social and ecclesiastical systems based on power.

> "Kingdom of God," a key term in the message of Jesus, is the biblical expression for the nature of God—unconditional and liberating sovereign love—in so far as this comes to fruition in the lives of men and women who do God's will, and is manifested in them. The kingdom of God is a new relationship of human beings to God, with as its tangible and visible side a new type of liberating relationship between men and women, within a peaceful reconciled society....

The kingdom of God is a new world of suffering removed, a world of completely whole or healed men and women in a society where master-servant relationships no longer prevail, quite different from life under Roman occupation. Precisely at this point Jesus turns especially to the poor....Jesus was aware that he was acting as God would do. He translates God's action for men and women....Jesus acts as God acts....To act as Jesus does is praxis of the kingdom of God and also shows what the kingdom of God is: salvation for men and women.[40]

Defining God

The kingdom can be a reality only at the cost of wholehearted conversion. It is the charism of a prophet to see to the heart of things. Only the starkest words can match his uncomplicated vision. The genuine prophet will speak a message of comfort, based on the faithfulness of God, but it will never be a comfortable message. That is why the demands of Jesus were uncompromising. He knew, better than any other, that sin was the greatest evil, the ultimate slavery. He discerned sin in selfishness and greed, in the seeking of status—most reprehensibly in the seeking of ecclesiastical power and privilege. He was conscious of sinful structures, political and religious. Indeed, he turned authority upside down (Mark 10:42–45). He took his stand on the Fatherhood/Motherhood of God. He believed that all men and women are children of this Parent, that all are sisters and brothers. He regarded sin as whatever conflicts with that family relationship of respect and love. Logically, then, his prophetic message was good news for the "poor." The poor were victims of the oppressive power of sin, an oppression mediated through sinful structures. This concern of Old Testament prophets found fresh urgency in Jesus' preaching.

In preaching the rule of God, Jesus was defining God. He proclaimed a God bent on the salvation of humankind. That is why he announced good news to the poor—the needy of every sort, the outcast. That is why he was friend of sinners, why he had table fellowship with them. And, in the long run, it was because Jesus had proclaimed a God of overwhelming mercy that he ended up on a cross. That God was unacceptable to the religious people of his day. That God is unacceptable to the professional religious of any day.

The Pilgrimage

Mark stands side by side with Paul as a stalwart proclaimer of a *theologia crucis*—a theology of the cross. And, congenial to modern Christology, the Marcan Jesus is the most human of any. Jesus is Son of God, that is, God-appointed leader of the new covenant people. He is "son of man"—*this man*—the human one who came to serve, the one faithful unto death. One who has come to terms with the cross (the meaning of his death) can know him and can confess him—like the centurion (Mark 15:39). His disciples did not understand him before Calvary. The Christian reader of the first century and of today is being challenged to come to terms with the love of God manifest in the cross of Jesus.

For Jesus, as for all of us, life was pilgrimage—at more than one level. What Luke had to say of the twelve-year-old is perceptively true: "And Jesus increased in wisdom and in years, and in divine and human favor" (Luke 2:52). His journey was not only from Nazareth to the Jordan, from Galilee to Jerusalem. It was, above all, a journey of faith. Jesus, who knew the Father as no other did, still had to learn what it was the Father asked of him at the end of all. He found himself face to face with the stark reality of the cross: "...not what I will, but what you will." While fully aware that, in everything he did and said, he revealed the true God, he was to find that his last word was to be the revelation of what Paul would call the "foolishness" of God. The man himself was the revelation; his life and death the medium of his message.

The pilgrimage of Jesus—*the* representative of our God—from a ministry of uninhibited love of humankind to death on a human-provided cross is the great and ultimate human pilgrimage. No banners there, no colorful procession—despite an ephemeral welcome (Mark 11:1–10 and parallel texts). Just disillusionment, shared by followers: "Jesus was walking ahead of them; and they were amazed, and those who followed were afraid" (10:32). They had caught the smell of disaster; the whiff was clear enough. Popular enthusiasm

114

had waned: Jesus was no messianic warrior but a pacifist for the cause of God. Yet, he had explicitly challenged the religious establishment by his criticism of Temple worship and of observance of Torah. He was a heretic. He had implicitly challenged Rome—by his outrageous notion of authority. He was a rebel. It did not matter that his challenge was totally peaceful and wholly marked by love. He was walking the most precarious walk of all: the walk of one who holds for love in face of those who acknowledge only power— whether naked or subtly disguised. That awesome, and awful, journey to the cross is comfort to all who have seen in Jesus of Nazareth the image of the invisible God. It is the consolation of all who have found in him the ultimate assurance that God is on *our* side.

Jesus had "set his face to go to Jerusalem" (Luke 9:51). Mark's Gethsemane scene (14:32–42) shows that he did not fully understand God's way, shows that he did not want to die. His Gethsemane decision was to trust God despite the darkness of his situation. He entrusted to God his own experience of failure: his endeavor to renew Israel was being brutally thwarted. His people had rejected him as they had, formerly, rejected his Father. His cry of God-forsakenness on the cross—"My God, my God, why have you forsaken me"—speaks the bitterness of his sense of failure. Contempt surrounded the death of Jesus. Archeology has shown that Golgatha, a disused quarry, was a rubbish dump. We have sanitized the Way of the Cross and the cross itself. The reality was sordid. And here we should remind ourselves that, as Christians, we know about God through the humanity of Jesus. We need to accommodate ourselves to the idea of a Supreme Being who can fully reveal himself in this manner.

Jesus had not set out from Galilee to embrace the cross. Throughout his ministry he had preached the rule of God—God as salvation for humankind. His last, involuntary, sermon was the most eloquent of all. The close of his earthly pilgrimage was to be his unequivocal proclamation of true divinity and true humanity. For the cross is God's revelation of himself. It is there he defines himself over against all human caricatures of him. God, in the cross, is a radical challenge to our hubris, our pride. There he is seen to be the *Deus humanissimus*—the God wholly bent on the salvation of humankind. No wonder that Paul can ask, in awe: "Since God did not withhold from us the most precious of all gifts, even the life of his own Son to give life to us all, can we not be certain that he would not possibly refuse us whatever else we may need?" (Rom 8:32).

The Lamb Who Was Slain

> One of the elders said to me: "Do not weep; the Lion from the tribe of Judah, the root of David, has won the right to open the scroll and its seven seals." Then I saw between the throne and the four living creatures and among the elders a Lamb standing as though it had been slain. (Rev 5:5-6)

In the Book of Revelation the emergence of the Lamb—John's definitive title for Christ—is dramatic even in the context of this dramatic book. The significant factor is that he is the *slain* Lamb. In his vision of the heavenly throne room, John had been bidden to look for the Lion of the tribe of Judah. What met his gaze was "a Lamb standing as though it had been slain." A surprise, surely— but ought we have been taken by surprise? After all, John's first characterization of Jesus Christ was as the one "who loves us and has loosed us from our sins with his blood" (1:5). Indeed, these very words are now caught up in the heavenly canticle: "...you were slain and by your blood you bought for God people from every nation..." (5:9).

When John proceeds to paint the power and triumph of the Lamb, he is clear and wants it understood that the decisive victory was won on the cross. He had made his own the conviction of Paul: "...we proclaim Christ crucified...Christ the power of God and the wisdom of God. For God's foolishness is wiser than human wisdom, and God's weakness is stronger than human strength" (1 Cor 1:23-25). It is precisely in view of the "foolishness" of God that John hears the heavenly celebration of the slain Lamb as one worthy to receive all power (5:21), as one worthy of honor side by side with the One on the throne (5:13).

In his vision John looked for the emergence of a Lion—and saw a slaughtered Lamb! What he learned, and what he tells his readers, is that the Lion is the Lamb: The ultimate power of God ("lion") is manifest on the cross ("lamb"). This is why "Lamb" is John's definitive name for Christ. Operating by the ultimate power of God, the Lamb conquers: "To conquer" (nikaō) is John's definitive Christological verb. To conquer, in the case of Christ and Christians, is to die. Throughout Revelation "conquer" never indicates vindictive action against the enemies of Christ or Christians. Jesus, silent before the Roman procurator, faithful unto death, won his victory.

The Lamb had won the right to break the seven seals. He went to the throne to receive from the hand of the One on the throne the scroll: a transfer of power (Rev 5). God had waited for an agent through whom his purpose for humankind would unfold. He had found him in the slain and risen Lamb. Our Almighty God manifests his might in the cross. In the cross, through the blood of the Lamb, God offers forgiveness and holds out salvation to all. There is only one answer to the evil that is sin, and to all evil. Violence can never be the answer. Despite the plagues of Revelation (plagues in vision only), it is not God's answer. Nothing but love, the infinitely patient divine love, can absorb evil and put it out of commission. The cross shows the earnestness of a gracious God, shows that there is no limit to his desire to win back a humankind gone astray. The Lamb as the manifestation, as the very presence of our gracious God, is worthy of honor and worship. He is worthy precisely as the slain Lamb, as the crucified One. In John's view, God's victory has been won on the cross. Jesus conquered through suffering and weakness rather than by might. Hence the paradox that, in Christian terms, the Victim is the Victor.

The New Jerusalem

The cross was not the end. Perhaps nowhere is this more firmly asserted than in the Book of Revelation. Two figures dominate Revelation: the Almighty One on the heavenly throne and the Lamb. The One on the throne displays his power in and through the Lamb who was slain. In his way, John makes the same point as Paul: "...we proclaim Christ crucified...Christ the power of God and the wisdom of God" (1 Cor 1:23-24). So fully is the Lamb the manifestation and the very presence of God that, at the end of all, in the New Jerusalem, in place of a temple is a single throne, "the throne of God and of the Lamb" (Rev 22:1). A marked feature of John's work is encouragement and comfort. His encouragement is paradoxical. His model is the Lamb *who was slain.* The Lamb has pointed the way to victory: The Victim is the Victor. The prize is eternal life.

What is eternal life with God? We, in our earthly existence, creatures of time and space, must perforce picture heavenly reality in terms of time and space. In Revelation 21:1-8 John has two central images. There will be a new heaven and a new earth (21:1). A creation that is, at last, utterly free of evil can only be *new.* Humankind is the summit of God's creation (Gen 1:26-31). His destined home for humankind was the garden of delights (Gen 2:15). There will be a new home for humankind in the new creation: a *city,* city of God, the new Jerusalem (Rev 21:2-4, 10-26). It is a heavenly city, yet a habitat of men and women. Heaven, however one may image it, must be a home for humankind—transformed humanity indeed, but a world of truly human women and men. It is a city without a temple. God and Lamb are there indeed, but not in the formality of a cultic setting. They dwell in the midst of their people.

Most dramatic of all is John's picture of the nations streaming into the New Jerusalem:

> The nations will walk by its light, and the kings of the earth will bring their glory into it. Its gates will never be shut by day—for there will be no night there. They will bring into it the splendor and wealth of the nations. (21:24-26)

They bring into it glory and honor—all that is worthy and lovely in human achievement. Though city of God, it is their city, true home of humankind.

John's glowing description is not only encouragement: It is challenge. We are summoned, here and now, to "lay aside every weight and the sin that clings so closely" (Heb 12:1; Rev 21:27). We are to look beyond evil to what is good in our world. We are to turn with confidence to the God who, though the One majestically seated on the throne, is the gracious God who wipes away every tear (Rev 7:17).

"See, I am coming soon" (22:7). It is an assurance that John's readers longed to hear. Life was not easy for them in the present. John's prospect of imminent tribulation augured much tougher times ahead. His promise to victors was all very well: The reality was that "conquering" meant dying! It was comforting to look to the One who was coming soon, "bringing his reward with him" (22:12). He was the one who had conquered by laying down his life. They, if they were faithful, would share his victory and his triumph. They look to his coming.

In the meantime, as they celebrate their Eucharist, they have his presence with them. They have the reminder of his victory and the assurance of his promise: "As often as you eat this bread and drink the cup, you proclaim the Lord's death until he comes" (1 Cor 11:26). They do not have to wait, bereft, for his final coming. Yet they long. "My desire is to depart and to be with Christ, for that is far better" (Phil 1:23). It is in their going to him that the Lord will come to them—and to us! *Marana tha.* "Come, Lord Jesus!"[41]

PAUL'S WORD OF HOPE

Paul had inherited the Hebraic eschatological schema. He envisaged two ages: the present age and the age to come. He came to regard the coming of Christ as the goal of God's plan of salvation. In his perception, Christ's coming, death and resurrection were the eschatological climax—"the fullness of time" (Gal 4:4), the beginning of "the resurrection of the dead" (Rom 1:4). But the end did not come. The eschatological climax was incomplete. What had happened was that the coming of Christ had disrupted the previous schema and required it to be modified. Where the older schema read: present age—end point [judgment]—age to come, the revised schema reads: present age—midpoint [cross/resurrection]—end point [parousia]—age to come. In other words, the two ages (present age/age to come) now overlap.

This means that for Paul those who have believed in Christ and received the Spirit live out their lives as Christ's between the mid-point and the parousia. That is, they live in the overlap of the ages, "between the times." Fundamental to Paul's conception of the process of salvation is that the believer has not yet arrived, is not yet perfect, is always *in via,* in transit. It is this which determines the experience of "being saved" as a process of "eschatological tension"—the tension between a work begun but not yet complete, between fulfillment and consummation, between a decisive "already" and a still to be worked out "not yet." It might be said that Paul's eschatology is backward-looking rather than forward-looking; at least it lies in the tension between the two. Paul's Gospel was eschatological not because of what he still hoped would happen, but because of what he believed had already happened. What had happened (resurrection and the gift of the Spirit) had already the character of the end and showed what the end would be like.

The Overlap of the Ages

The beginning of chapter 5 of Romans marks a major transition. Up to this point, Paul's focus was on faith; now the focus shifts from faith to *hope.* The affirmation of hope confronts that "overlap" situation of present Christian life. On God's side, for those justified by faith, the new age has dawned. But, in their bodily life, they remain fixed in the old age, afflicted by weakness, suffering and death. Righteousness—having a right relationship with God—has set them on the way to salvation. But the goal is still a matter of hope (8:23-25). They are challenged to hearken to the Gospel in such a manner that hope lives and is fostered.

A clearly defined "inclusion" marks off the section contained in chapters 5-8 of Romans. Broadly, it is constituted by 5:1-21 and 8:14-39; more sharply by 5:1-11 and 8:31-39. The explicit theme of both passages is *hope,* a hope founded on the peace brought by God's justification (5:9; 8:31-34) and attested by the Spirit (5:5;

8:14-15, 23-27). It is a sturdy hope that faces and endures the reality of suffering (5:3-4; 8:17-18, 35-39). It is a hope that rests upon the love of God shown in the gift of the Son on our behalf while we were sinners. Now that we are God's friends, that hope must surely see us through to the end (5:6-10; 8:32). That hope is challenge to live out the fact of righteousness, to reach that goal of salvation. The basis of hope is firm indeed: "God proves his love for us in that while we were sinners Christ died for us" (5:8). We were "sinners"—weak, without moral capacity. Christ died to rescue us from that state. This showed, unmistakably, God's personal love for us. Christ's self-gift in love is the historical expression of the eternal love of God. It is a love that knows no limits because it is the love of the God who "justifies the ungodly" (4:5)—those alienated from God. More simply, God is the Judge who *acquits* the *guilty*. This paradox challenges the propriety of imaging or speaking of God as Judge at all.

SUFFERING

In Romans 5:3 Paul dares to characterize suffering as ground for boasting. He can declare that suffering can give rise to hope. This is more than making a virtue of necessity. Suffering not only underlines the painful reality of life in the "overlap" but is a reminder of death. Paul was keenly aware that the process of salvation is an ongoing experience not only of life but also of death. Death is at work in the believer as well as life. In the overlap, believers are in a divided state. In their belonging to this age, they are dying; in their belonging to the age to come, they experience the life-giving Spirit. It is not surprising that the metaphor of "death" is prominent in Romans 6.

IN CHRIST JESUS

In Romans 5:12-21 Paul had insisted that the free gift of grace in Christ Jesus had far outweighed the ravages of sin. Then, in response to the false inference of 6:1 ("Should we continue in sin in order that grace may abound?"), he declared that we have "died to sin" (6:2). By this "death" he means that we have escaped, once for all, from the tyranny of sin. He is not denying the practical situation: the continuance of sin in the lives of believers. He formulates

121

the basic principle: what ought not be. He pointed to the baptism of Christians as implying involvement with Christ in his death. In baptism one is "buried" with Christ, sharing the finality of death. Yet, the death of Christ was not "final": Christ was raised from the dead. Christ had "died to sin, once for all" (v 10); he had broken the dominion of sin and death. Because Christ's burial was a stage on the way to resurrection-life, believers, too, "baptized into Christ Jesus," are conformed to him in death and in risen life. Conformity is the key. As Christ had "died to sin," the "concrucified" believer has put to death the "body of sin," the complex of involvement with a world under sin. In other words, one has broken free from slavery to sin. This leads to a further conformity: with the *life* of Christ— "If we have died with Christ, we believe that we will also live with him" (6:8). As, for Christ, death led to life, so baptismal death leads to newness of life. In Christ Jesus the believer is "dead to sin and living to God" (v. 11). This factor, even "between the times," marks the new age. It is a life, free from the rival lordships of sin and death, lived wholly under the lordship of God. It is a life that must be embraced: "So you also must consider yourselves dead to sin and alive to God in Christ Jesus" (6:11).

> Paul summons believers to adopt the attitude that responds to this new situation. As Christ is "dead to sin" and now "lives to God," the same mindset must characterize those who share his new existence, those who are "in Christ Jesus" *(en Christō Iēsou)*. This phrase represents Paul's most characteristic way of developing the life of believers "within" the risen Lord as all-compassing "sphere" or "milieu" of salvation. Since Christian life is encompassed totally "within" Christ in this way, the "no longer" and the "once for all" aspect of his personal existence and "career" apply— or ought apply— equally to them. They can no longer live "in (the power of) sin because they live in (the sphere and power of) Christ Jesus" (v. 11)....It is not so much a matter of imitating Christ or even of simply allowing their lives to be "conformed" to the pattern of his (cf. v. 5). At base, it is a matter of allowing the attitude or "mind" of Christ, and obedient "living to God" characteristic of his earthly and risen life, to "well up" within them because of their existence "in Christ" (cf. Phil 2:5). They are called, in short, to allow the risen Lord to live out his continuing obedience to

the Father in them as in his own extended person or "body" *(sōma)*. This is the heart of Paul's ethic for the new era of grace.[42]

Sharing Christ's Sufferings

Paul has, beyond Romans, developed the theme of a sharing in Christ's sufferings as an aspect of Christian life. He regarded suffering as an integral part of the eschatological tension—of life "between the times." The crucifixion of Jesus made it inevitably such. "I have been crucified with Christ" (Gal 2:19) is not a once-for-all event because what is meant is that "the world has been crucified to me and I to the world" (6:14). In effect, this means: I am still hanging with Christ on that cross. For, in this age, before the parousia, Christ remains in me the crucified one. Here and now I am conformed to the crucified Christ. My conformity with the risen Christ is yet to be: "...if we have died with Christ, we believe that we will also live with him" (Rom 6:8); we have been buried and raised with him (6:4). This is not all. Between the "with him" of the already ("buried with him") and the "with him" of the yet to be ("raised with him") there is a further "with him." With and in Christ, the first born, we are children of God and joint heirs with Christ—"...if, in fact, we suffer with him so that we may also be glorified with him" (8:17). The "with him" of the in between time is to suffer with him.

The twofold aspect of the process of salvation—experience of the power of Christ's resurrection and the sharing of his sufferings—is expressed again in Philippians 3:10: "I want to know Christ and the power of his resurrection and the sharing of his sufferings by becoming like him in his death." In the simplest terms, the process of salvation is "becoming like Christ." But this must mean that the conformity is to Christ crucified as well as to Christ risen.

The upshot of it all, and the comfort, is that, as Paul saw very clearly, the transforming power of the cross works *in* human weakness. "We have this treasure in clay jars, so that it may be made clear that this extraordinary power belongs to God and does not come from us" (2 Cor 4:7). This is spelt out in detail in 2 Corinthians 12:9–10

> He said to me, "My grace is sufficient for you, for power is made perfect in weakness." So, I will boast of my weaknesses, so that the power of Christ may dwell in me. Therefore I am content with weaknesses, insults, hardships, persecutions and calamities for the sake of Christ; for whenever I am weak, then I am strong.

The lesson is clear. The weakness of the believer does not prevent the power of God from being effective. Divine power does not obliterate or set aside human weakness. What Paul perceived as the mark of grace was experience of power in and through bodily weakness. Human weakness was no denial of divine power. Rather, as an unavoidable complement of divine power in the overlap of the ages it was, indeed, an integral part of the process of salvation. It was in this light that Paul regarded suffering. He was not proposing it as, in any sense, an end in itself. He would have had little patience with a later ascetical bent that fostered a cult of suffering.

Life in the Spirit

In the bleak passage Romans 7:14–25 Paul portrayed the helplessness of life without grace, a situation not relieved but exasperated by law. In that regime of sin it was impossible not to sin. In the new era of grace it is possible *not* to sin. While living "according to the flesh" is still a hazard for believers, one now has the freedom to say no to sin and yes to God. Tensions remain in Christian life; choices have constantly to be made. But there is no longer the utter helplessness of the old regime: "Wretched man that I am! Who will rescue me from this body of death?" (7:24). There is now the Spirit, source of transforming power.

In Galatians 5:19–26 Paul had graphically portrayed the diametrically opposed lifestyles of two "types": those who "live according to the flesh" and those who "live according to the Spirit." The flesh person, enslaved to sin, is cut off from God, reaping a dire harvest (5:19–21). The Spirit person is wholly at one with God, tranquilly gathering the "fruit of the Spirit" (5:22-23). There, rhetorically, is the stark contrast. In the messy reality of the overlap of the ages the situation is more complicated. The tension is always with us.

The two powers of flesh and Spirit remain competing realities in the current experience of the believer. The reason is made clear in Romans 8:11—"If the Spirit of him who raised Jesus from the dead dwells in you, he who raised Christ from the dead will give life to your mortal bodies through his Spirit that dwells in you." The "if" is crucial. Spirit persons are still in danger of succumbing to the weakness of the flesh and its desires. In the tension of the between times they must be on their guard. They must maintain and foster openness to the Spirit and be resolute in resisting the lure of sin in the flesh.

In a manner reminiscent of the Two Ways of Deuteronomy (Deut 30:15,19) Paul offers his readers a stark choice between "death" and "life": "If you live according to the flesh you will die; but if by the Spirit you put to death the deeds of the body, you will live" (Rom 8:13). He then continues in a style more in line with the theme governing Romans 5-8 overall: the hope of glory held out for all believers despite the sufferings of the present time (8:14-25). In verse 17 he stresses the filial status of the Christian—but not as an end in itself. "Children" are destined to be "heirs," an inheritance fixed on a firm christological basis: "...if children, then heirs, heirs of God and joint heirs with Christ..." To share the glory, however, into which Christ, as prime heir of God, has already entered, one must, necessarily, share his sufferings: "...if, in fact, we suffer with him so that we may also be glorified with him." In short, if hope is so firmly a characteristic of Romans 5-8, it is a hope mysteriously conjoined with the experience of suffering.

There is a practical and pastoral corollary to this tension of a life lived in the experience of conflict between flesh and Spirit. There has been a persistent tendency to confuse means of living *in* this tension with means of *escaping* it. In Paul's view there is no means of escaping the tension. The simple fact is that believers do live in *this* age, an age not yet fully free from the power of sin and death. They still suffer the weakness of the flesh. While they do indeed experience the power of Christ's resurrection, it is within that weakness. The life they live is, paradoxically, in and through "death"—as a sharing in Christ's sufferings. The presence and experience of conflict is an assurance that there is life. Absence of conflict would signal the absence of the Spirit, the triumph of death.[43]

The Love of God

The great peroration of Romans 8:31-39 celebrates the victory of God's love. It is vulnerable love: God "did not withhold his own Son" (8:32). Having committed himself wholly, he will not tolerate any hitch to his saving purpose. Trials and sufferings of this age will not frustrate love of Father and Son for us (8:35-36) "We are more than conquerors through him who loved us" (8:37): This love of Christ was concretely shown in his giving himself up to death on our behalf. Paul himself lived his Christian life "by the faith of the Son of God who loved me and gave himself for me" (Gal 2:20). He was happy to put his trust wholly in the faithfulness of Christ.

The remarkable declaration of Paul's certainty of salvation (Rom 8:31-39) is a summary of the whole first part of Romans—and, it might be said, of Paul's Gospel in general. It tells us that God's love is *like this*. It assures us that here is the God who has laid claim to us and has given us a claim on him. We learn at once who God is: He is God *for us*. It is as good a definition of God as we might hope for. God is the loving God who created us and called us to be his daughters and his sons. The question of verse 32—"He who did not withhold his own Son, but gave him up for all of us, will he not with him give us everything else?"—can have one answer only. The giving of his Son shows, beyond doubt, that God is in deadly earnest. Father and Son were prepared to go to any length to save humankind from itself. God gave his Son without any precondition: God took the risk. The death of the Son was, at the deepest level, a sacrifice made by God.

There is a division of opinion as to how verses 33-34 should be punctuated. The preferred choice here is of two questions with ironical answers. Who can bring a charge? God—who justifies! It is really another way of putting the question of verse 31—"If God is for us, who is against us?" Can we imagine that the God who, in our helplessness, has, at such a cost, taken his saving initiative is now going to be our Judge? And who will condemn us? Christ Jesus who died for us, who intercedes for us! Again it is another way of putting a question: "Who will separate us from the love of Christ?" Christ's love for us is dramatically manifest in his sacrificial death and in his efficacious intercession. Tribulations and distress cannot separate us from that love of Christ. It is evident that the suffering in question is especially suffering that comes in the service of "the Gospel." It follows, though, that no trials of our human lot can come between the Christian and that unyielding love.

With the Jewish and Hellenistic worlds of his day in mind, Paul insists, for those who believed that angelic beings had influence over humans, and for others who believed in astrology, that none of these "forces" had any effect on God's love for us. The simple fact is that nothing in the whole of creation—which is God's creation—can come between us and God's love for us, concretely expressed in the unqualified giving of his Son for our sake. It has been finely said: "There is no arguing with such a certainty. Either you simply don't believe it or you recognize it as the word of God."[44]

MERCIFUL TO ALL

Death has been swallowed up in victory. Where, O death, is your victory? Where, O death, is your sting? (1 Cor 15:54)

Death is the inevitable close of human life on earth. Death is passage from this world of time and space to the eternal world. Death brings encounter with God. It is the moment of truth. If one's image of God is decisive for the manner in which one lives one's life, it is crucial in determining how one faces the prospect of death. Death may come in many ways. It may be sudden and painless. It may come at the close of prolonged and painful illness. It may be the result of human cruelty. It is salutary, and comforting, to keep in mind the anguished cry of Godforsakenness:

127

"My God, my God, why have you abandoned me?" It is wise to recall the prayer of Gethsemane: "If it be possible, let this cup pass from me." Jesus did not welcome a cruel death; he shuddered at the prospect. He found, in earnest prayer to the Father, the courage to face it. Yet, shattered by the seemingly hopeless failure of his mission, and in physical agony, he felt the absence of God. His prayer, wrenched from him, was lament—a cry to the One who could deliver him from suffering. When one is in great pain, it is not easy to pray. It is more natural to cry out. This is the pattern of Old Testament lament. That was the way of a crucified Jesus. "My God"; that absent God was still his God. Jesus learned that God had not abandoned him.

Failure?

More and more one comes to appreciate why Paul had reached the firm intent to preach the message of the cross: "I decided to know nothing among you except Jesus Christ and him crucified" (1 Cor 2:2). The death of Jesus is our assurance that God is not aloof from human death as he is not absent from any aspect of human life—of life, in short. Yet, that death had marked Jesus as historically a failure. He was executed on the order of a Roman provincial official: An alleged troublemaker in that bothersome province of Judea had been dealt with. The incident did not raise a ripple in imperial affairs. Yet history has shown that this execution was an event of historic proportions. Its ripples flow stronger than ever two thousand years later.

Let us be clear about it. The Romans and the Jewish Sanhedrin had effectively closed the "Jesus case." The aims and message of Jesus, and his life itself, had ended in death. His prophetic voice had been muzzled. This is failure. The question is: Why had Jesus been silenced? It was because he, unflinchingly, had lived and preached God's love for humankind. That is why he had table fellowship with sinners, why he sought to free women and men from the tyranny of religion, why he, at every hand's turn, bore witness to the true God. He might, in face of the threatening opposition, have packed it in and gone home to Nazareth. That would have

128

been real failure. But he would not be turned from witnessing to God's love. They might take his life, but to his last breath he would witness. What Jesus tells us is that failure is not the last word. That is, as God views failure. From God's point of view, in the fate of Jesus, there could be no question of failure. Yet, Mark has taught us that a *sense* of failure, even for Jesus, is a grievous human experience.

The career of Jesus did not end on the cross. Just as the death of Jesus must not be detached from his life, his resurrection must not be detached from his career and death. Because he was raised from the dead, Jesus holds decisive significance for us. Because of the fact of his resurrection we know that meaningless death—and, often, meaningless life—has meaning. Jesus died with the cry on his lips, "My God, my God, why have you forsaken me?" The sequel was to show that God had not abandoned Jesus. We have the assurance that he will not abandon us. While, unlike his immediate disciples, we do not follow the steps of Jesus from Galilee to Jerusalem, we do join his human pilgrimage from birth to death. His word of promise is that we shall follow him beyond death to share his rest (see Heb 12:2). We shall know fully our *Abba* at last and become wholly his children.

The death of Jesus, marked by an anguished cry, met a Father's response of welcome. It is understandable that our human imagining should set death in a context of judgment. It is, indeed, the moment of truth. The point is, it is God's truth, not ours. That brilliant judgment scene in Revelation says it all (see Rev 20:11–15) with its "books" and "the book of life." The resurrected dead were "judged according to their works, as recorded in the books." That would seem to be it, then. If this were all, we have justification by works! Happily, there is that "book of life." Salvation is of God alone—as it was for Jesus. God has the last word. His book is the book of life.

Merciful to All

Our God, who spoke the first, creative, word is determined to have the last word. This, of course, is as it should be. That word has to be good news. What we have perceived of the sheer graciousness of God would urge us to see it so. Israel, notably in prayer of lament, had discerned this. There is robust faith and firm hope in the plaintive "Why?" and "How long?" There is a holy impatience to it. It springs from the conviction that God can do better, much better, than he is doing. There is nothing mean-spirited in the repentance of Israel. Confession of sin carries the assurance that sin has been forgiven. The prophets have consistently perceived word of divine mercy behind warning and threat—beyond even divine chastisement as they reckoned it. The question, then, arises: Will God's word of mercy eventually embrace all of humankind? A vital factor here is human freedom and God's utter respect of our freedom. Precisely because of the freedom factor it is impossible to say, definitely, that salvation will be universal. But, when one focuses on God, then one may appropriately hope for the salvation of the whole human race. It is not a vain hope. It carries an impressive scriptural warranty.

Universal Salvation

If salvation means fellowship with God and blessedness of eternal life with God, universal salvation means that all human beings will eventually be redeemed by God's gracious love—a love displayed ultimately in Jesus Christ. On the other hand, a limited salvation view assumes that only those who, in this life, acknowledge the true God and, in the Christian Scripture setting, confess Christ as Lord will finally be saved. Both views—limited salvation and universal salvation—are found prominently in both Old Testament and New Testament. A stream of texts maintains that final salvation is limited (e.g., Isa 26:20-21; 66:15-16; Matt 25:31-46; John 3:36). Another stream suggests or affirms universal salvation (e.g., Isa 66:18-23; John 3:17; Rom 11:32-36; 1 Tim 2:3-4). In some cases, both views are juxtaposed (e.g., Isa 66:15-16, 18-23; John 3:17; 3:26).

Here it will suffice to list some further texts that, arguably, point toward universal salvation: Psalm 86:9; Isaiah 25:6,8; 52:10; John 12:32; 1 Corinthians 15:22,28; Philippians 2:10-11; 1 Timothy 2:3-4; 4:10; Titus 2:11. Somewhat surprisingly, the view is present throughout the Book of Revelation. See Revelation 1:7; 5:13; 14:6-7; 15:3b-4; 21:3, 24-27.[45] Arguably the weightiest text of all in favor of universal salvation is found in Paul. In Romans 9–11 he addresses the problem: How could God's people have failed to recognize God's final Messenger? Throughout the chapters he wrestled with a humanly incomprehensible situation but never loosed his grip on his conviction of God's utter faithfulness—"...the gifts and calling of God are irrevocable" (11:29). At the end, he committed the whole matter to God and declared, in words that had little to do with the forced logic of his argument up to now: "And so all Israel will be saved..." (11:26). A remarkable statement. Then, Paul took a truly giant step: "For God has imprisoned all in disobedience so that he may be merciful to all" (11:32). His declaration has to be seen in contrast to the unrelieved picture he had painted in Romans 1–3: All humankind stands under sin, cut off from God. But, then, that backdrop was designed to highlight the incredible graciousness of God (to be presented in chapters 5 through 8).

A celebrated Matthean passage, the last judgment scene (25:31-46), with the fearsome words, "Depart from me you cursed, into the eternal fire," would seem to challenge Paul's hope. Rather, we are to understand Matthew's scene as myth—a symbolic form of expression couched in narrative that is not intended to be historical. It deals with realities that transcend experience—in this case the reality of definitive encounter with God. In effect, the "last judgment" is warning: It primarily relates to one's conduct in the present. One is challenged to live in such a manner that, should it occur, one would not be caught unaware. We are being taught how we should prepare for the "coming" of the Lord, prepared for our meeting with him. The "last judgment" is taking place in my life here and now. The "books" are being written. But has my name "been written in the book of life since the foundation of the world" (Rev 17:8)? There is the true judgment.

HEAVEN AND HELL

"Last judgment" conjures up visions of heaven and hell. The terms *heaven* and *hell* are, obviously, human words—and the accompanying imaginings are all too human. Theologically, in the context of the "last things," what the terms signify is the reality of human decisions for good and evil and consequent human possibilities. Contemporary theology, on the basis of human freedom and of God's total respect for freedom, regards hell as a possibility. God alone knows if a human being can definitively choose evil—and only in such a case is there the possibility of "hell." Still, the prospect of heaven and hell is salutary, pointing up the seriousness of decision in the present.

Heaven and hell are symbols, but they are not on the same level; they are asymmetrical affirmations of faith. The basis of "eternal life"—that is what *heaven* means—is living communion with God. God is source of that bond of life which is already a reality during earthly life, a bond that cannot be snapped at death. Living communion with the living God abides beyond death. So there is heaven. There can be no hell on the same level. For, if living communion with God is the foundation of eternal life, the absence of such communion is the basis of noneternal life. There is no longer any ground of eternal life. The evil have excluded themselves from communion with the living God—excluded themselves from life. They no longer exist. To reject God is to reject being itself; it is to opt for nothingness. Hell is the condition of nonbeing; it is not a place or state. A mistake of the past has been to set good and evil on the same level. Evil, as distinct from good, is not something positive; it is the absence of good.[46] There is nothing in evil that can mark it out for eternal life. Through its inherent emptiness the wicked world disappears by its own logic into absolutely nothing. Edward Schillebeeckx puts it:

> So there is no future for evil and oppression, while goodness still knows a future beyond the boundary of death, thanks to the outstretched hand of God which receives us. God does not take vengeance; he leaves evil to its own limited logic! So there is in fact an eternal difference between good and evil, between the pious and the wicked....God's unassailable holiness consists in the fact that he will not compel anyone to enter the kingdom of heaven as the unique kingdom of liberated and free people. The "eschaton" or the ultimate is exclusively positive. There is no negative eschaton. God, not evil, has the last word. That is the message and the distinctive

human praxis of Jesus of Nazareth, whom Christians therefore confess as the Christ.[47]

There is no negative *eschaton*. This, it seems to me, is a better way of describing what we have been considering under the rubric "universal salvation." The trouble with the expression "universal salvation" is that it might be taken in a manner that trivializes the deadly conflict between good and evil in our history and cheapens our view of God's mercy and forgiveness. God, not evil, has the last word. God's saving purpose for humankind—the *Eschaton*, the End—is salvation. There is no negative *eschaton:* God does not will damnation. For that matter, "positive *eschaton* only" might be a better way of stating what "universal salvation" is meant to express. Salvation is offered to all. But God is God of freedom; he will not compel. Whether any person, faced with Infinite Love, can choose to embrace evil—and, at some point, the choice must be stark; anything less would be unworthy of our God—we do not know. What must surely follow from the character of our God is this: There is one way and one way only in which a human person may not be saved. That is by cold-blooded rejection of a PARENT who is sheer LOVE. One leaves salvation firmly where it belongs. God and Lamb alone know what names are inscribed in the book of life (see Rev 20:11 -15; 17:8). And, appreciating something of the foolishness of God, one rather suspects that the names of all humans will be read there.

Conclusion: Becoming Human

Christian is one who is called to a way of life. Most of us are initiated into this way of life in our infancy, or we reach a time when we make a conscious decision to live, seriously, or with some seriousness, a Christian life—or we drift away from that pattern. If we do insist on calling ourselves Christian, we do so for a variety of reasons.

Our age does seem to be firmly stamped by secularization. It does not seem to have much concern for God. At the same time, there is a thirst for meaning in life. This desire is a quest for God, even when it is not recognized as such. On the other hand, when God is consciously sought, the quest may be misdirected. The god envisaged may not be truly God.

There is a basic yearning for wholeness—for authentic humanness. For the believer, God is God of humankind. God is found where there is goodness and a striving for the liberation of humankind. This calls for a critical assessment of religion. God is present in our history; he is found in the most ordinary aspects of human life. The path to God is the path of authentic humanness. Our secularized world has such need of God that our contemporaries may be more likely to find the true God than people of a more "religious" age.

Because they perceive a Western world characterized by rampant secularization, many Christians tend to take a poor view of our world. In truth, a pessimistic Christian is a contradiction in terms. We ought to be incurably hopeful: "In the world you face persecution. But take courage; I have conquered the world!" (John 16:33). What is encouraging is the realism underlying this assurance. The promise is uttered in the setting of a world that, in essence, was little different from ours.

134

It is refreshing to hear a theologian who finds hope and promise where many can discern only ground for discouragement. Edward Schillebeeckx maintains that in the contemporary world the question of God is the most open question of all, that the way of God is the most exciting challenge. God is on the side of humankind. The noblest task of humankind is to reveal the true God. God is to be seen in whatever is authentically human. This is why God was supremely present in the human person who "went about doing good" (Acts 10:38). Our world not only needs God but may be poised to acknowledge and manifest God. And this because our world may be conditioned to acknowledge that God is pure gift—our ultimate luxury.[48]

Salvation

A yearning for salvation is a profoundly human desire. It is, in one form or other, at the core of every religion. We humans know ourselves to be flawed. We set goals before ourselves and fail to reach them. Time and again we find, to our dismay, that we are more frail than we had feared. We may seek to fool ourselves but cannot sustain the deception. We are unwhole but long for wholeness. We look for salvation.

What is salvation? It is perceived in various ways; it has been made to mean many things. It has been made to seem ethereal, unreal. It has been presented as transcending humanness, even as denying humanness. This is tragic because salvation means nothing other than attaining perfect humanness. We *are* human beings, created in the image of God; we are meant to *image* God. Our destiny is to be human—as God understands humanness.

The author of Hebrews had thoroughly understood that the salvation of humankind could not be salvation *from* humanness; it is salvation *of* our humanness. Hence his insistence on the humanness of Jesus. Salvation cannot be something outside our humanness; this would be no salvation at all. What has, in fact, come to pass is something intensely moving: God, in Jesus, reaching into our history of suffering and brokenness. "It was fitting that God, for whom and through whom all things exist, in bringing many

ground of growth. Coming to terms with oneself does not mean settling for mediocrity; it is not remaining where we are. We might apply the parable of the wheat and the weeds (see Matt 13:24-30): "Let both of them grow together until the harvest..." (13:30). The parable is word of admonition: the final decision is at the harvest and is God's alone. But "wheat" and "weeds" are human beings. The parable is a challenge to look at oneself, to see oneself. And if I recognize that I am a "weed," I am not fated to remain such. I can become "wheat." Indeed, I am invited to become "wheat." It is what God desires of me. But I cannot do it on my own. I can do it by trusting myself to the care of God. And by responding to the urging of God.

The Call

The invitation of God, the call of God, comes to me not in signs and wonders but in the web and woof of every day. Here is where I find my God: where I am now, in what I do now. There is indeed a call that has—or is meant to have—the quality of prophetic call, such as the call to religious life. Of its nature, it is relatively rare. One is concerned here with the general invitation to live as a child of God. God's call to us is not something rare. It is a summons to the special task of being human and ordinary. That is challenge in plenty. Someone has said that holiness consists in doing ordinary things extraordinarily well. A sad by-product of religion is departmentalization. True, there are seasons and places that are "sacred." But this does not mean that all the rest is "secular." All that is good, all that is authentically human, is sacred. Sin is precisely denial or betrayal of the good, the truly human.

Acknowledgment of a gracious God does not imply a lowering of standards. When I have convinced myself that God knows me so much better than I know myself, when I have simply and wholly accepted that God loves me for myself as I am now and at every moment, then I will hear his invitation. Awareness of my shortcomings will not inhibit or depress me. It will spur me to do better, to be better. Response to the comforting assurance of God's love will not bring complacency but a willingness to respond. It

138

will not matter if response is not as generous, as wholehearted as I could wish. God will not ask of me more than I can deliver. And, if I fall, I can pick myself up again. Experience of my frailty will not dishearten. It will make me more appreciative of a love that is wholly undeserved. I need not feel helplessly alone—because I am not alone.

Freedom

If I have really come to acknowledge that prodigal Father of Jesus' parable (see Luke 15:11-32), that foolish God of Paul (see 1 Cor 1:18-25), then I can taste freedom. I will be free of stifling preoccupation with self, free of crippling feelings of guilt. I can dare to be more open with others. And, perhaps most liberating of all, I will be free of restrictive bonds of religion. Worship and observance will find an important place in my life. My worship of a gracious God will not be duty but glad response. And observance will not be marked by subservience to rules and law but by practical acceptance of a lifestyle in keeping with my status as child of a beloved Parent. Response will not be calculated nor tinged by fear. It will be free. And life will be worth living.

This is no soft option. Christians may be children of God but only on condition that they understand what this means and live what it demands. The way of being a child of God has been firmly traced by Jesus himself: "Anyone who wants to be a follower of mine must renounce self, take up one's cross and follow me" (Mark 8:34). Jesus delivers a challenge, the challenge of his own way as Son. Being a disciple is a serious business. Yet, taking up one's cross is not at all to say that suffering is something Christians should seek. Jesus did not seek suffering; Gethsemane is proof enough. But suffering will be part of Christian life as it was of Jesus' life.

"To be a follower of mine"—the comfort is that the following can be in tiny steps. God is patient. His challenge is invitation. Faithfulness to one's way of life, concern for others in whatever manner, the caring gesture, the kind word—these add up. There will be heroes—the few; there will be those whose way will seem ordinary and drab—the many. Even in the things of God we are prone to measure by worldly standards. The Lord will not overlook the painful decision, the unspoken sorrow, the secret suffering. There are surely many more saints than those whom we honor as such.

Being Christian

There is more than one way of being Christian. One need but look to the rich pluralism of the New Testament. There is a corresponding variety of spiritualities. It is a temptation of organized religion to construct a map with the "orthodox" road to salvation clearly defined. Alternative routes are, in this view, at best dead ends. At worst they lead in quite the wrong direction. There are those who find comfort in the map and are helped on their way by it. There are others who trudge along, grimly. They find that though the map may be clear, the road turns out to be an obstacle course. There are some who find the map helpful in spots but who prefer to wander and explore. These people take religion seriously but preserve a sense of humor. They smile at self-importance and posturing. They are ready to follow their hearts. They are not awed by logic because they know that God, the supremely free, is wondrously illogical. They are not browbeaten by law, because they know that God is the God of freedom. Perhaps best of all, they do not take themselves too seriously—because they know that God takes them with utter seriousness.

NOTES

1. Sandra M. Schneiders, "Spirituality in the Academy," *Theological Studies* 50 (1989): 684.

2. It is notorious that gender-exclusive language is problematic in the extreme in reference to the deity. The pronoun is the snag. In the current state of the language it is just not feasible to avoid it consistently. Realistically, that pronoun has to be "he." Of course, one is wholly aware that God is not male—nor female for that matter!

3. Dermot A. Lane, *Keeping Hope Alive* (Dublin: Gill & Macmillan, 1996), 71.

4. Ibid., 71.

5. Ruth Page, *God and the Web of Creation* (London: SCM, 1996).

6. Ibid., 49.

7. Ibid., 43–44.

8. Ibid., 64.

9. See note 2.

10. Edward Schillebeeckx, *Jesus in Our Western Culture* (London: SCM, 1987), 8.

11. Ibid., 7.

12. Paul Gallico, *Thomasina* (Middleton, U.K.: Penguin, 1987), 146.

13. Edward Schillebeeckx, *God Among Us: The Gospel Proclaimed* (New York: Crossroad, 1983), 94.

14. See John F. Craghan, *The Psalms* (Wilmington, Del.: Michael Glazier, 1985), 140–45.

15. Baruch 1:15–3:8; Ezra 9:6-15; Nehemiah 1:5-11; 9:6-37; Tobit 13:1-8; Sirach 36:1-17; Esther 13:9-17; 14:3-19; Judith 9:2-14; Daniel 3:26-45; 9:4-19.

16. See below, pp. 90–92.

17. See below, pp. 130–131.

18. Terence E. Fretheim, *The Suffering God* (Philadelphia: Fortress, 1984); Wilfrid Harrington, *The Tears of God* (Collegeville, Minn.: Liturgical Press, 1992).

19. See Harrington, *The Tears of God,* 26–37.

20. Walter Brueggemann, *Hopeful Imagination: Prophetic Voices in Exile* (Philadelphia: Fortress, 1986), 38.

21. Wilfrid J. Harrington, *Hold On to Hope: The Foolishness of God* (Dublin: Dominican Publications, 1998), 13–35.

22. Jurgen Moltmann, *The Trinity and the Kingdom of God: The Doctrine of God* (London: SCM, 1981), 47.

23. H. Wheeler Robinson, *The Cross in the Old Testament* (London: SCM, 1960), 47. This book groups three essays: "The Cross of Job" (1916), "The Cross of the Servant" (1926) and "The Cross of Jeremiah" (1925). All are splendid: beautifully written by a fine and sensitive scholar. One cannot read Robinson on Job and fail to gain a deeper appreciation of this biblical masterpiece.

24. Ibid., 31.

25. Ibid., 32.

26. Ibid., 30–31.

27. Harrington, *The Tears of God*.

28. Schillebeeckx, *Jesus in Our Western Culture*, 28.

29. "The concept of God in [the great councils of the fourth and fifth centuries] is different from that in the Old and New Testaments. In them we have a Greek concept of God which does not stand in any direct relationship to our earthly time and space. There too, a quite different image of humanity is used from that in the Bible. Within this conceptual framework of humanity and God (which needs to be criticized in the light of the Bible) these councils, precisely in order to remain faithful in a Hellenistic milieu to the New Testament Jesus Christ, were obliged to speak as they did. Authentic Christians were speaking here—but at the same time they were thinking Greeks. What they did secured and saved the New Testament confession for us. But this does not mean that we must accept the philosophical and anthropological presuppositions of these Greek councils (or a particular model of the incarnation) as the condition for a living and unabbreviated faith in Jesus confessed as the Christ. These councils, from Nicaea to Chalcedon, show us little of the vulnerable man Jesus who also suffered on the cross. In these councils the individual Jew Jesus of Nazareth faded away to give place to the 'one human nature,' ahistorical. Moreover what these councils meant to say was essentially hardened and even distorted in catechesis, preaching and theology. And in church tradition they often functioned as a source of understanding faith almost independent of the New Testament, standing by themselves: they were even used as a more important source than scripture." Ibid., 45–46.

30. See Wilfrid J. Harrington, *John: Spiritual Theologian: "The Jesus of John"* (Dublin: Columba Press, 1999).

31. See Wilfrid J. Harrington, *Mark: Realistic Theologian: The Jesus of Mark* (Dublin: Columba Press, 1996).

32. Turid K. Seim, *The Double Message: Patterns of Gender in Luke-Acts* (Edinburgh. T. & T. Clark, 1994), 162.

33. See Wilfrid J. Harrington, *Jesus and Paul: Signs of Contradiction* (Wilmington, Del.: Michael Glazier, 1987), 57-61, 148-62.

34. Seim, *The Double Message,* 260.

35. See Wilfrid J. Harrington, *Luke: Gracious Theologian,* "The Jesus of Luke" (Dublin: Dominican Publications, 1997), 74-86.

36. Claus Westermann, *Lamentations: Issues and Interpretation* (Edinburgh: T. & T. Clark, 1994), 81- 82.

37. Claus Westermann, *Prayer and Lament in the Psalms* (Edinburgh: T. & T. Clark, 1981), 275.

38. Harrington, *The Tears of God,* 34.

39. G. M. Tucker, "The Role of the Prophets and the Role of the Church," in D. L. Petersen, ed., *Prophecy in Israel* (London: S.P.C.K., 1987), 173.

40. Schillebeeckx, *Jesus in Our Western Culture,* 19-20.

41. See Wilfrid J. Harrington, *Revelation,* Sacra Pagina 16 (Collegeville, Minn.: Liturgical Press, 1993); *Revelation: Proclaiming a Vision of Hope* (San Jose: Resource Publications, 1994).

42. Brendan Byrne, *Romans,* Sacra Pagina 6 (Collegeville, Minn.: Liturgical Press, 1996), 193.

43. For the preceding treatment of Paul I am much beholden to Brendan Byrne, op.cit., and James D. G. Dunn, *The Theology of Paul the Apostle* (Edinburgh: T. & T. Clark, 1998).

44. C. H. Dodd, *The Epistle of Paul to the Romans* (London. Collins, 1959), 160.

45. See Harrington, *Hold On to Hope,* 59-64.

46. Thomas Aquinas, *Summa Theologiae,* Ia. q. 48, art. 5.

47. *Church: The Human Story of God* (London: SCM, 1990), 138-39.

48. Schillebeeckx, *Jesus in Our Western Culture,* 5-6.

Other Robert J. Wicks Spirituality Selections

Simply SoulStirring by Francis Dorff, O. Praem.
Transforming Fire by Kathleen Fischer
Living the Hospitality of God by Lucien Richard, O.M.I.